Magic Bullets by Savoy

Magic Bullets

by Savoy

Magic Bullets
By Savoy

Published by Classic Books Publishing, Christoph Lymbersky, Luetkensallee 41, 22041 Hamburg.

Disclaimer:

Publication date: July 2009, Hamburg, Germany

Registered with:

Copyclaim: #10000967

ISBN-Agentur für die Bundesrepublik Deutschland in der MVB Marketing- und Verlagsservice des Buchhandels GmbH
Bibliografische Information der Deutschen Nationalbibliothek
Die Deutsche Nationalbibliothek verzeichnet diese Publikation in der Deutschen Nationalbibliografie; detaillierte bibliografische Daten sind im Internet über http://dnb.d-nb.de abrufbar.

Front Cover Picture: © Classic Books Publishing & Love Systems Inc.
Interior Pictures: : © Love Systems Inc.
Text Layout: : © Classic Books Publishing

When ordering this title, use ISBN: 3941579347 and the EAN-13 is 9783941579347

Contents

Preface

"Everyone here eats tacos..."

Those were the first words I heard Savoy say during the in-field portion of my Mystery Method bootcamp. Until then I had been... skeptically unconvinced. During the first day at seminar, I thought it sounded great, but wondered whether it was the real deal or not. Then I watched Savoy approach a group of women with those ridiculous words, immediately get attraction... and then end up alone with an attractive woman. It was enough to let me know I had things to learn from this man.

I later became an intern while I was still in college and the "office" was Savoy's living room. Back then it was just Misschievous, Savoy and I. We went for Indian food, worked out together and argued over why he so foolishly loved the Philadelphia Eagles. I also met Neil Strauss and many of the other world's greatest pickup artists. I was really happy to be there.

And I saw what Savoy was capable of firsthand. I saw a LOT of different women leaving his house in the morning when I showed up for work... Sometimes two. ;)

It started to crystallize in my mind that there were greater possibilities for me. I had been okay with girls after my program, but it still hadn't really clicked that I could achieve THIS lifestyle. Savoy took me under his wing and showed me how to do it. The guy was an amazing resource and teacher. He was proof that even a board game-playing dork from Newfoundland with horrible taste in football can have insanely good and consistent game... And it rubbed off. With his help, I began to live the life I'd been dreaming of and different girls started leaving MY house every morning as well.

Then the company grew from 3 of us to 4, to 5 and moved to Los Angeles. I watched firsthand as Savoy turned us into the leading in-field, cold-approach dating company in the world. I watched as reporters from all over the world started calling. I watched a company grow exactly as Savoy had planned it all along from day one. We taught thousands of students and changed tens of thousands of lives; in the process, the top guys became Love Systems. Through all this time, Savoy has been one of the greatest mentors and friends I have ever had. I considered myself lucky to have him as a boss and as a friend who I still call for dating advice to this day.

The book you are about to read is not a magic bullet in the sense that reading it will completely change you overnight. The title is meant to be ironic. But what it will do is give you the map and the skills to get to the place where you want to be, through a combination of hard work, dedication and the application of the wisdom you are about to read. If you commit to putting what is in these pages into practice you WILL attain the relationships and lifestyle of your dreams.

I honestly can't think of anyone better to learn from. For those of you who know my reputation, the knowledge in this book was the path that led me to where I am today. It should be read a couple of times to get the full benefit because there is just so much to learn...

If there is any "magical" way to get better with women, be it attracting, building or maintaining great relationships, it's contained within these pages... so in that sense, it is the closest thing to a magic bullet around. Read it, internalize it and apply it with dedication and passion, and I hope that all of you reach the goals that you set out to achieve as you enrich and transform yourselves with the insights contained in this book...

SINNcerely,

Jon (Sinn)

Introduction

Magic Bullets is an ironic title. A central theme of this book is that there is no magic bullet to get the women of your dreams. There is no one single thing, or even ten things, you can do that will all of a sudden allow you to reach your full potential. It won't always be easy, but if you read and study this book and other resources that *Love Systems* has to offer, you'll get there.

I've spent years teaching men how to improve their success with women. Since 2004, I've been President of Mystery Method Corp., which was the gold standard in this field and then its top instructors and I founded Love Systems. I've worked closely with other masters, men who go by names like Sinn, The Don, Mystery, Tenmagnet, Badboy, Cajun, Braddock, Cortez, Sheriff, Mr. M, and Brad P (most people in this field use pseudonyms). I've seen Tyler D teach, and been out with Style (a.k.a. Neil Strauss) more than a few times.

These guys are all masters. They have developed working systems that allow them to have high-quality women in their life.

But these systems are not what make them good. None of these guys was an overnight success (and I wasn't either). Most of them have six things ("The Fundamentals") in common:

1. Most of them spent months, or even years, in a conscious process of self-improvement.

2. All of them had to study and understand female psychology, usually first from books and then "in the field" (in live interactions with women).

All of them had to develop social intuition so they could recognize and predict patterns of social behavior.

All of them developed a lifestyle that women found attractive.

All of them had to develop skills that allowed them to make their systems work - skills like humor, storytelling, or kissing.

All of them have been on many dates, even if they call them something else, and know how to use dates to their advantage.

So here's the dirty little secret…

If you've taken care of the fundamentals, any reasonable system can work. The Don could use Brad P's system and get great results. Style has used Mystery's system and done well. I've used a couple of different systems before making my own.

A system for attracting women is like a strategy for a basketball game. Some teams shoot a lot; others pass more and wait for a great scoring opportunity. Some teams run back quickly on defense; others rebound aggressively. But if you have players who are good at the fundamentals (which in basketball means things like shooting, running, and dribbling) any reasonable strategy can work.

Just like if you have good dating fundamentals, many different systems can work. Sure, one system might fit you slightly better than another, just like in basketball a team with big players might use a more physical strategy than a smaller but faster team. Badboy does his thing and not mine because it's slightly better for him. But if he had to, and if he had the time and the motivation to practice it, he could attract beautiful women with mine, or anyone else's.

Of course, it's possible to have a basketball strategy that won't work, even with the best players in the world. The national team for the United States in the 2004 Olympics is a perfect example of this.

The same goes for dating. I recently read a book in which the author tells men to approach women seated in restaurants with the line: "A beautiful woman like you should have a beautiful evening. Do you mind if I join your table?" That's not going to work no matter how good your fundamentals are.

And if your fundamentals were truly good, your social intuition and your under-standing of female psychology would have stopped you from making such a bone-head approach in the first place. We'll cover female psychology in Chapter 3 and social intuition (one of the eight key attraction switches) in Chapter 7.

Devil's Advocate

Let's play devil's advocate for a moment. If it's true that it's the fundamentals that are important, how can it be that someone can learn a dating system and immedi-ately get better results?

Just like a basketball team with a decent strategy will beat a team with no strategy, a man who learns a workable dating system will do better than he did before he had one. Often, such a man will convince himself that he has learned "the secret" and has the magic bullet for succeeding with women. This belief will actually help him, by giving him confidence, until he hits the inevitable dead end that comes from not improving the fundamentals. In my years of experience in dating science, I have never – nor have my colleagues ever – seen a man become truly successful with women without being able to handle the fundamentals.

But a good devil's advocate wouldn't be satisfied yet. He would want to know why, if all of the above is true, so many people are still obsessed with dating systems?

Here we have stumbled onto the myth of the One True Path: the idea that you should pick a guru and follow his system, focus on his system, and ignore every-thing else.

The One True Path fallacy is seductive, because it fits in nicely with human psy-chological patterns, especially in males. Men naturally want to believe it. Say some guru tells you 10 things that you need to do to get a woman to go out with you. Well that's sure simpler than looking at the complicated woman across from you and trying to figure out what's going on in her mind. And it works for the guru, so it must be good, right? And it's a secret that you know that most men don't, so that makes you feel powerful as well.What makes the One True Path so dangerous is that it can explain away your failures in a way that doesn't challenge your faith. For ex-ample:

> You do the 10 things the guru says and you don't get the girl? That just means you haven't mastered them yet. You need to practice more.

> You lost the girl when you did one of the 10 things, but the other three seemed to go okay. Great! You're getting better at three of the 10. You just need to practice that one.

> Your friend succeeds with a woman by doing something that your guru doesn't teach or recommend? Ignore it. You're learning the guru's system so you can date even more attractive women than your friend meets – women like your guru gets.

The One True Path fallacy also exists because it's easy to communicate. It's easy to tell you to do these 10 things and you'll get what you want. I can do that in a paragraph. It's much harder to account for the what-ifs and exceptions, as I do in this book. Some of the most powerful, if misguided, ideas in the world do not toler-ate ambiguity. Facism, Fundamentalism, and Communism are all One True Path fallacies. However, dating science does not respect absolute laws like physical science does, no matter how tempting it is to think that it does.

Systems

So after all of this, why is there even a system in this book?

For one thing, it makes a convenient organizing principle. For example, it's a good way of keeping material on how to start a conversation (Chapter 5: Opening) in a separate chapter from material on what to do next (Chapter 6: Transitioning). This is even though the information presented in the chapters describing the Emotional Progression Model (our system) would appear no matter what system we happened to be using or what we titled each chapter.

Moreover, you do still need a system, whether it's your own or someone else's. And some systems clearly don't work, so at least if you're using this one, I'll know that you're not going up to women at restaurant tables and trying to sit with them with cheesy pickup lines. Even some famous dating gurus' systems suffer from being too specific. For example:

They only work for certain types of men (age, looks, personality type, etc.).

They only work with certain types of women.

They only work in certain situations. The system that we teach at Love Systems – and that is explained here – is both more flexible and more specific. Flexible in that it works for a broad range of men, with a broad range of women, in a broad range of situations. Specific in that we also drill down to specific types of situations, types of women, and types of relationship outcomes. I want you to have a dating system that works for you, not just for some guru with a clever marketing strategy.

The system here is not one I invented out of my head – that would be irresponsible. If I invented something purely out of my own experiences, I could hardly claim to have seen it used by enough different men, with enough different women, in enough different situations, that I could be confident it would work for anyone who bought this book. Of course, my own originality is stamped throughout this book, as are the unique ideas of the best dating coaches in the field. However, when you come across something that I do myself or have seen others do that hasn't been tested rigorously in this way, it is labeled and identified as such.

The system in *Magic Bullets* was developed by the masters in the field, especially by the top instructors of *Love Systems*. It has evolved and been dramatically improved over the past two years based on insights that our instructors have made and taught, and based on the way we've seen most people actually use the science of dating successfully. I'm excited to present it to you, backed up by the fundamentals that will let you reach your full potential.

I also want to share with you a bit about my approach in writing this book. There isn't, or at least there shouldn't be, any self-referential flattery, beyond personal examples to help explain a point. I'm not out to convince you that I know what I'm talking about by talking about myself. It's a waste of your time and it's irrelevant. The only thing that matters is how the material in the book works for you.

If you're curious about my personal experiences and adventures or those of other instructors and our students, I invite you to check out our blogs and The Attraction Forums. They're free, they're public, and their web addresses are listed in Chapter 25. You can also find a lot of reviews (positive and negative) of this book, our instructors, and our training on *The Attraction Forums*. While you're there, why not post your own?

While the book is (I hope) orderly and easy to understand, the subject matter is not. Dating and relationship behavior is complex and full of contingencies and exceptions. In every case in which there was a tradeoff between an elegant model and a lucid analysis of a topic, I have opted for the latter. Accordingly, this book is not where you will find a bunch of new words, new acronyms, or complexity for complexity's sake. Instead the book is designed with only one purpose: to help you succeed.

To that end, I'd like to invite you into a dialogue. If you have any comments, ideas, or experiences from reading the book that could help subsequent editions serve its purpose even better, I'd love to hear from you.

Savoy

Savoy@LoveSystems.com

Acknowledgments

More people contributed to this book than could possibly be named here. As I've said elsewhere, dating science is a cumulative science, and we all build on the ideas of those who came before us.

In particular, I've learned a great deal from dating coaches I've worked with in the past few years.

My biggest influences are fellow instructors with Love Systems, the world-famous (some would say notorious) organization that helps men succeed with women. In particular, I've learned a lot from Jon (Sinn), Scott (The Don), Chris (Tenmagnet), Pete (Sheriff), and Thompson (Future). These men were at the core of Mystery Method Corporation since 2005, and many remain the star instructors with Love Systems today. All of them contributed ideas to the first edition of Magic Bullets and have aspired to continue learning and pushing the frontiers of knowledge since. As Love Systems has expanded and grown, we've trained multiple new masters, who in turn have gone on to dramatically expand the world's store of knowledge on how men can succeed with women. Foremost among these are Mr. M, Braddock, Soul, Fader, Rokker, and Cajun, and their contributions are evident throughout this book.

I did not want to write a great Love Systems book; I wanted to write a great psychology and tactics book for men who wanted more choice, more results, and more success with women. I learned from everyone in my path who had something to contribute. I learned a great deal from Badboy and Cortez from Badboy Lifestyles (a competitor) and Brad P from Brad P Presents (another competitor). I learned from Tyler D, who years ago gave me my first glimpse into the world of possibilities I never suspected existed. Even three years ago he was a fountain of knowledge, and seeing him approach beautiful women and instantly generate attraction inspired me to develop my own skills and push them as far as they could go. I learned from Mystery, who popularized the idea of a sequential model and many techniques that stem from it.

Most of all, I've learned from women – those I've approached, those I've dated, and those who indulged me through endless hours of conversation about their dating and relationship experiences.

In particular, I learned from Misschievous. I've known her since before this adventure began, and even though we're no longer involved, she inspired me to build something that women can contribute to and be a part of. If this book is dedicated to anyone, it's to her.

I also want to thank everyone who reviewed drafts of this book and provided feedback. Sinn and The Don contributed important ideas and perspectives throughout the book and I owe them a debt of gratitude for their patience and insight. The book would not be the same without their contribution.

DJ provided generous and insightful suggestions that improved the chapter on Storytelling. Frank Denbow, Christina Levy, Suzanne Weiss, and many other volunteers helped edit individual chapters; if you're one of them and have not yet been appropriately thanked, get in touch.

Finally, I want to thank mondayMEDIA Graphics for the design of the book, proofreading each chapter and invaluable suggestions throughout the first edition.

For VAH/The Mystery Method Readers

Some of you might have read the published book The Mystery Method or the electronic book The Venusian Arts Handbook. These represent the thinking of the Mystery Method Corporation up to about 2005. As President and Program Leader of Mystery Method Corp. from 2004, I was proud of my role in developing these products. Even today, they are light-years ahead of most other published material to help men to succeed with women.

If you are not familiar with either of these works, you can skip this chapter (or read on, if the evolution of dating science interests you).

If dating science is a science at all, it is a cumulative one. What was great in 2005 might still be very good today, but we've also moved forward. Men who have actively researched and tested different ways of attracting women have identified and fixed problems with earlier systems. Whereas Mystery Method Corp. between 2004 and 2005 was inspired by Mystery, the people running and teaching Mystery Method Corp. programs since then we were able to create a better and deeper approach that worked for virtually every man, not just for one, very unique, person. Over time, the top instructors wanted a vehicle that would express this more directly, and thus Love Systems was born.

Still, respect for the cumulative principles of dating science requires us to build on the work of those who came before us wherever possible, and only to replace when necessary. Thus, I have deliberately re-used as much of the terminology of The Mystery Method as would fit the Love Systems model. Approaching still means approaching. Comfort still means comfort, and so on. How we approach a woman, or how we build comfort with her, has changed and developed dramatically. But the words used to describe the process are useful markers and a head start for those familiar with The Mystery Method. It would only be a disservice to experienced readers to start calling "Comfort" something different, like "Intimacy" or "Rapport" or "Emotional Connection" just for the sake of using new words.

Listing all the changes and additions in Magic Bullets would be another book in itself. But for our experienced readers, I'll give a selection of them here:

Magic Bullets includes...

New understandings of each phase of the model

Six types of openers: Magic Bullets does not shy away from Direct or Challenging openers, and shows how even a Functional opener can work.

The concept of Transitioning: This is an entirely new phase. Mystery Method Corp. used to advocate going straight from Opening into Attraction. Other instructors and I made it work because we intuitively knew what kinds of Attraction material work when delivered as a non-sequitur immediately after the Opener. When we realized that we were "transitioning" into the Attraction phase, it led us to the concepts of a normal vs. a single-subject conversation (see Glossary) and to the Transitioning Phase.

Five systematic ways of conveying Attraction material: The book identifies and analyzes the five different ways that a woman can become attracted to you – from observing you to you telling her about yourself – and how to use each one. We also identified the eight key "attraction switches" and have a much broader (and different) understanding of what is attractive to women and why.

A new model for Qualification: Qualification used to be taught as a discreet phase that had a defined end-point and was taught with the bait-hook-reel-release model using very hard Qualifiers like: "so what do you have going for you more than your looks?" Mostly through Sinn's work, we have an enhanced understanding of Qualification. Releases are not always necessary. You have a broader range of Qualifiers available to you. And the phase doesn't end; it blends into Comfort.

Breakthroughs in Comfort: It's a bad pun, but this book presents Breakthrough Comfort (formerly Advanced Comfort) as well as an understanding of how to build comfort without having to do anything to actively create "isolation."

Seduction without LMR or freezeouts: Intellectually, there was nothing wrong with the previous approach; however, many people interpreted our discussion of LMR and the use of freezeouts as making Seduction an oppositional process between men and women. We don't want that. We don't want women to be or feel manipulated into having sex. And through an understanding of state breaks, how they work, and the Avoid / Blur / Distract model of dealing with them, we don't have to make women feel this way.

The Relationship Phase: Previous material did not include significant treatment of what comes after you first have sex with a woman. Magic Bullets introduces the new phase called "Relationships." It also covers the 6 major relationship types (from Traditional boyfriend/ girlfriend relationships to Friends with Benefits), relationship management, and how to use the time before you have sex with a woman to lead to the type of relationship you want.

A general change in philosophy

Bypassing using pickup "lines" or other people's material: We teach you how to make your own.

Underlying theory based on culture and an improved understanding of evolutionary biology: While we had the right idea in general before as to what worked, we were a bit hazy on why it worked. See Chapter 3 for more on this.

Understanding Attraction and Qualification as continuous processes: Previously, the process of attracting a woman and then qualifying her had specific starting and ending points. We've improved this. The bulk of Attraction still usually happens before Qualification, and the bulk of Qualification takes place before you start building Comfort, but both Attraction and Comfort levels need to be refreshed and maintained throughout your interaction with a woman.

Treatment of different social contexts: We now explicitly recognize how social circle, work, day game, strip clubs, and so on affect the social dynamics of a situation and how you have to adjust your strategy with a woman accordingly. Chapters 13-15 deal with this.

Detailed chapters on the fundamental skill set (as described in the Introduction to this book):

Physical progression: Formerly called "kino." Covered with new insights in Chapter 16.

Dates: Chapter 17 covers good dates, bad dates, 10 tips to an effective date, who should pay, and when and how to escalate sexually.

Storytelling: Some of the most detailed analysis of storytelling in the field of dating science can be found in Chapter 18.

Non-verbal communication: Body language and tonality are crucially important and are addressed in Chapter 19.

Kissing: When to kiss. How to get her to kiss you. Very important, and covered in Chapter 20.

Fashion: Your clothing choices can dramatically improve your looks. They also convey your identity. Chapter 21 explains how to do both.

Winging: Chapter 22 provides a detailed breakdown of the theory and practice of meeting women when out with skilled friends (your "wingmen").

Phone Game: Chapter 23. closes the skills section with a discussion of how to talk to a woman on the phone, how to arrange dates, and when to call.

Chapter 1: How to use this book

1

How to use this book

This is a long book. And it's going to be read by a lot of different people who have different skill levels with women (what we call "game") and different needs and goals. For this reason, I've designed the book so that it doesn't have to be read all at once. You don't even have to read the chapters in order.

Each chapter is designed to stand on its own, as a useful reference, and most chapters make specific references to other chapters for related material.

I do recommend you read the book in order at least once, but here are some other options if you're impatient:

If you're on your way out tonight and want quick tips, go to Chapter 2: A Simple System you can use tonight.

If you want a step-by-step guide to meeting desirable women you don't know and developing a romantic or sexual relationship with them, start with Chapter 4: The Emotional Progression Model, and the subsequent explanation of each of its seven stages in Chapters 5 to 11.

If you've got your overall approach down and want to apply it to different social contexts – female friends, women you work with, "day game," strip clubs, etc., then Part III of this book (Chapters 12 to 14) is for you.

If your concern is around tweaking specific aspects of your game – anything from your body language to what to do on the first phone call – then you want Part IV (Chapters 15 to 22).

If you've read the published book The Mystery Method in bookstores, or bought the Venusian Arts Handbook online and want to know what's new, flip back a few pages to introductory Chapter IV.

What you are reading now is the product of literally tens of thousands of individual interactions with women, by myself and other current and former Love Systems instructors. We systematically generate, test, challenge, and refine our theories, and they are enriched by innumerable different men using our ideas and reporting on their results. But that doesn't make anything in this book a physical law or scriptural commandment. All rules are meant to be broken, and you will get more in the long run from experimenting and building on this material than from applying it unthinkingly. It's the spirit of experimentation and testing that brought us to this level, and it's that spirit that will help you get the most out of reading it.

Chapter 2: A Simple System you Can Use Tonight

2

IN THIS CHAPTER:

A Simple System you Can Use Tonight

Magic Bullets is a long book. Really long. You're not going to get through it all in a day, or even a week. And it's designed to be something that you keep coming back to, over and over, as your experiences using the material allow you to learn more from it each time. It's designed that way. If you're new, you probably won't grasp all of the advanced implications of what's in this book until you've been going out for a while and using the material. If you're already advanced, your eyes will skip quickly through the more introductory material and focus on the more advanced material in each chapter.

But there's a third possibility. It might be Friday night, you're going out, and you just bought this book.

Maybe you have a couple of hours to skim through it – if you do, I recommend it – or maybe you don't.

Let's say you just have 20 minutes. You don't need to learn how to deal with every possible situation. You don't need to know why Magic Bullets works. You don't need to know what to do on dates, what to do when you call her, or how to manage her relationship expectations. You don't need to know how meeting women through friends or at work is different from meeting them at a bar, or how to meet women during the day, or how to attract an exotic dancer. This stuff (and a lot more) is all in the book, but it's not for tonight.

What you need is some quick information that will get you started with a couple of the more common types of social scenarios that you're likely to run across at a typical bar or nightclub.

This will necessarily be very basic and in no way represents the full depth of what you will find in Magic Bullets. It's not a summary and it's certainly not a "best-of." I picked this material because it's the easiest to learn in 20 minutes and go out and use tonight.

When You First Arrive

- Act like you own the place. Walk in confidently. Keep your head high, walk slowly, don't be afraid to take up space, and smile. How you enter a venue can set the tone for how people react to you the rest of the night.

- If you're alone, approach a group right away (I explain how to do this in a moment). If you're with friends, have fun and joke around with them. Do not wander around to "check out the bar" or scan the area with your eyes looking for attractive women.

- Be louder; almost every sober guy in a bar or club is too quiet.

- Stand up straight, make eye contact, and don't lean in to hear a woman. In fact, never lean in.

- Body language and tonality are covered in detail in Chapter 19.

The Emotional Progression Model

- Our model follows a woman's emotional progression from first meeting you to being in some form of relationship with you, even if it's just friends with benefits. The next six sections give a couple of tips for each phase of the model. (The 7th - on relationships - is one you don't have to worry about tonight.)

- *Key insight #1*: You create mutual attraction before you build comfort. Put another way, you hold off on the "what's your name?" and "what do you do?" questions as well as the really deep conversations until it's obvious that you are both interested in each other.

- *Key insight #2*: She needs to be showing that she is interested in you before you can show her that you are interested in her. Don't worry; we're about to show you how to get a woman interested in you.

- Chapter 4 explains the model in detail.

Meeting (OPENING/APPROACHING)

- The simplest way to meet women at a bar is usually to stay near the bar area. Don't get drunk.

- When you see a group of two or three women together, pretend to "spontaneously" notice them and ask them a question like one of these:

- "I'm planning my friend's birthday party next Friday and I'm trying to decide between an 80s theme and a jungle theme. What do you think?"

- "My friend keeps getting anonymous emails from a secret admirer but he thinks he knows who it is. Should he say something?"

- Ask the question like the situation is really going on, not like you're taking a survey.

- These are the beginnings of "opinion openers." In Chapter 5, we explain how to use them, what comes next, and we go over six other types of ways to start a conversation with a woman, including much more direct methods.

- Always start talking to a woman within a few seconds of seeing her. This is important. Don't stare. Don't lurk. Lurking is creepy. Creepy is bad. Nothing will turn a woman off more than creepy. Any time that you don't want a woman to be interested in a man, imply that he is "creepy." Approach right away.

- You can approach other groups (including women by themselves, larger groups, groups with men in them, groups sitting down, etc.) but a couple of women together at the bar is the easiest to get started with.

- Approaching is dealt with extensively in Chapter 5.

Transitioning

- Once they've started talking about your friend's birthday or secret admirer for a few seconds, cut them off by noticing something about them. Yes, actually interrupt them. What you notice can be something simple like "You look like you'd be a schoolteacher." Or, it can be a longer, more playful piece such as:

    – "Alright it seems that you [pick one woman at random] are the good one and you [the other woman] are the bad one. And that's okay. One of you can be my angel and the other can be the devil. Like we'll roll down the street, one of you on each arm, we'll make all the other women jealous, and every time there's a decision to be

made, you guys can whisper in my ear and we'll
see who's more tempting."

The point of the transition is to move from a narrow, one-subject conversation that will eventually exhaust itself (like your friend's birthday or secret admirer) to a normal conversation about all sorts of things. Observing something about the people you're talking to – especially if it's done in a humorous or intriguing way – is a great way to do this.

There are also other types of transitions (this one just happens to be easy to use), and we cover them all in Chapter 6.

Important note: Don't compliment anyone or ask personal questions yet. Don't worry about why this is; we don't have time for that now (it's explained in Chapters 4-11).

Attraction

- Now that you have a normal conversation going, your next goal is get attraction from the woman you are interested in. This makes for one of the longest sections in the book (Chapter 7). For now, here are a couple of techniques:

    o Tease her (playfully; don't be mean) – give her a nickname.

    o Tell good stories. Funny is usually good. Tell your stories as if they are emotional journeys, not recitations of facts.

    o Don't do anything that would be interpreted as hitting on her. – Be entertaining, without seeming to try too hard.

- Keep the idea in your head that you've been with more beautiful women than the one(s) you're talking to, and that you don't need anything from them; you're just having a good time. Don't say this and don't be negative, but let these thoughts guide and influence your behavior. A challenging man drives women crazy. Why Challenging is one of the eight attraction triggers and how to be challenging is explained in Chapter 7 (Attraction).

- Up to and including this point you will be doing 90% of the talking. Don't let silence happen. Keep talking.

- Never leave a group because you "ran out of things to say." Say anything. Even the most boring thing in the world is better than awkward silence. Forcing yourself to say something – anything – will get you used to improvising and handling social pressure.

- As you get good at this, you should be consistently getting some signs of attraction from her.

- Chapter 7 goes into a lot more detail on the five basic ways of creating attraction and the eight things you want her to know about you (attraction triggers). Some examples of signs of attraction are: touching you; laughing at your jokes; or staying and talking to you for 20 minutes or so. There are about fifteen other important signs, but for tonight those are the three big ones.

- When you're getting a few signs of attraction, tone it down. You don't need to tease her as much anymore. You can give her sincere compliments now. This is explained in the next section on Qualification.

Qualification

- When she is giving you signs that she is interested in you, switch gears. Now you can indulge your curiosity about her. You can ask her "screening questions" like: "So, what do you do for fun?" When she tells you things about herself that you are attracted to, compliment her on them.

- Three compliments are usually enough. And make her earn them; she should have to talk about things that are genuinely interesting to you.

- Once she's done this, you can say something like "when I first met you I wasn't sure about you.

- Now that I get to you know you, you're pretty interesting."

- Use the information she gave you by answering your screening questions to begin building rapport and looking for commonalities.

- Chapter 8: Qualification covers this process in more detail; it's a tricky one. There's a ton more to it than I can fit here and it takes some practice, but these tips should get you through tonight.

Comfort

- This is where you can roll out all of the usual "What do you do?" and "Where are you from?" questions.

- Concentrate on getting to know each other across a wide variety of topics as opposed to talking about one subject in detail.

- Don't make your conversation into an interview. Use statements instead of questions whenever possible. Prompt her to tell you about herself by telling stories yourself.

- You should already have begun touching her playfully before this stage, but now it's time to initiate more intimate touches. Start out with playful pushing, tapping, thumb wrestling, etc., and then move into more intimate stuff like hand holding and kissing... It should be a smooth, upward transition that is comfortable for both of you.

- The Comfort phase is where you decide what to do next: take her home (Seduction) or get her phone number. These are our next two topics.

- Chapter 9: Comfort covers this in detail, including what to do if her friends are still around, how and when to get alone with her, and how to make her feel completely connected to you.

Seduction

- Seduction is about being alone with her and progressing toward sex.

- Your big obstacle in Seduction is "state breaks" – jarring interruptions when a woman has to consciously think about the possibility that she is on the road to having sex with you. These include: going home with you, moving into your bedroom, undressing, and so on.

- Chapter 10 goes over the three basic ways of dealing with state breaks (avoid/blur/distract); for tonight, focus on distraction. When something is about to happen that will engage her logically in this way, do something else that will take her attention away. For example, when you take her home, talk non-stop. Don't talk fast or appear nervous, but don't let a moment of silence come in.. Keep her mind occupied with your words. Your monologue will distract her from the fact that she is coming home with you.

- As for sex itself, you're on your own. This isn't that kind of book.

Getting Her Phone Number

- Make sure you get her number; don't just give her yours.

- You can get a phone number anytime in or after the Attraction phase, but it's best to wait until Comfort. We explain why in Chapter 23 (Phone Game).

- Make specific plans for what you two will do that is interesting and doesn't involve dinner and a movie.

- Stay for at least 5 minutes after you get her number.

- Chapter 22 covers how to get a woman's phone number so she'll answer when you call and what to do in the first phone conversation.

Before you go out

You probably don't have time to make major changes to your wardrobe right now, but here are a few things you can do with what you have:

- Untuck your shirt. Zap nose hairs and unibrows. Women notice.

- Junk any khakis or golf shirts you might be wearing.

- Put on one interesting item – a pendant, a ring, an unusual jacket, something that stands out and will get people talking to you.

- Fashion and grooming are covered extensively in Chapter 21: Fashion. It's not the kind of fashion you'd find in GQ; it's what's been proven to work for getting the attention of beautiful women who you meet out in public.

General Rules to Remember

- Don't introduce yourself to women even if you've been talking for a few minutes. When a woman asks your name, it's a sign she is interested in you.

- Don't ask her about her personal information in the first fifteen minutes you are talking to her. (15 minutes is an approximation; the actual timing depends on what emotional signs she is giving up and is covered in Chapters 7 to 9.)

- Don't compliment her on any aspect of her appearance or what she is wearing.

- Keep a very playful vibe; you can't look like you are taking things too seriously.

- When you encounter resistance, change her mood, not her mind.

- Be non-reactive to things that aren't the results you want. Being non-reactive is very attractive to women. Just enjoy yourself and don't seek specific responses from her.

- Have fun! If you're not having fun, she won't have fun.

Again, this isn't a summary of the book of a best-of. It's definitely not the best way to succeed with women, and once you read the rest of the book, you'll probably put this chapter aside. But if you're going out now, you need something, and this is a quick, simple plan that will get you started.

3

IN THIS CHAPTER

- Basic Psychology
- Quick primer on evolutionary biology
- Evolutionary biology today
- Evolutionary biology for women
- Foundations
- Attributes
- Congruence

Basic Psychology

If you're a man, the odds are that you know very little about female psychology. Actually, it's worse than that. The odds are that most of what you think you know is wrong.

Why is this? I'll let you in on a secret here. Men are bombarded with false or misleading messages about female psychology because there are powerful societal forces that give a misleading perspective on the world, as opposed to accepting it for what it is.

Am I saying that there is a giant conspiracy to cover up the true nature of 52% of the world's population but I just happen to have seen through it? Of course not. There's no conspiracy. But most men's lack of understanding of women is real and is caused by a bunch of factors that form a powerful nexus.

First up is that many women don't understand themselves. Try this as an experiment. Ask a woman what a man should do to impress her. She'll probably respond with some combination of taking her to a nice dinner, maybe a walk on the beach, maybe flowers, a few compliments, really listening to her, and so on. Now try doing that. When you come home alone after a peck on the cheek and the "let's just be friends" talk, don't say I didn't warn you.

Most women do not know or do not want to admit what actually attracts them.

Now are women lying to you? No. All of these sweet romantic things do have their time and place. Usually this time and place is after a woman is already attracted to you. A woman head over heels in love with you would love to be taken to a nice dinner and brought flowers. A woman who is trying to decide about you would be turned off. I'll explain why in a bit.

Another factor is that some of the stuff that tends to attract women – all of the stuff described in Chapter 7 like having higher perceived social status, having other women around you, teasing them or even making them feel momentarily insecure – isn't nice. It's not what women want to feel attracted to.

Most women actually don't even know that this stuff attracts them. This is because emotions A) are not conscious choices and B) don't come with instruction manuals. When someone is attracted to someone else, they realize it because they have an emotional response to that person. Men are the same way. When you're interested in a woman, it isn't because you took out a notepad and calculator and said to yourself "She's got nice hair... she's fun and doesn't seem weird... I like her body... she's interested in the same things as I am... I think I'm attracted to her!" No. You are attracted to someone because you feel that emotion. Now, you may know yourself well enough to know what qualities some women have that tend to make you feel attracted to them, but that's different from deciding to be attracted to someone because she has those qualities.

On the other hand, most people don't know themselves perfectly. You may think you are attracted to someone because you find her beautiful, but what actually triggered that attraction might be that you were feeling particularly lonely or sexual at that moment, or your friends might have commented on how attractive she is, or her perfume reminded you of your first crush, or whatever.

These examples all pertain to men. Now go ahead and multiply this for women, who feel all basic emotions (except anger) much more strongly than men. Women get attracted, and then try to explain, or rationalize, to themselves and others why they feel the way they do. Another reason why you won't always get great advice from women about attraction is that societal messages get in the way. A lot of women are deeply attracted to men with money (and a lot aren't). Some of these women admit it. Others feel guilty about it, and pretend, sometimes even to them-selves, that they like a man who "just happens" to be rich because they like his sense of humor or style or his values.

Another factor getting in the way of understanding female psychology comes from the influence of politics and the law. In the twentieth century, most developed counties passed laws mandating the equality of men and women. Legal equality is of course a good thing. But there is a very big difference between believing that men and women should generally have equal civil and employment rights, and believing that men and women actually are identical outside of their physical differ-ences.

If you were raised or went to school in a "politically correct" environment, you might actually believe this. In which case, you would also believe that any behavioral differences between men and women are attributable to societal influences. Under this theory, people are rewarded if they behave in ways consistent with society's view of their gender and punished if they do not, and most people choose to con-form.

I'll demolish this myth in a moment, but let me first rescue the grain of truth that actually exists within it. Societal influences actually do work in this way. For exam-ple, men who do not play a dominant role in their relationships with women are often snickered at for being "whipped." Assertive women get thought of as "bitchy" while assertive men are considered to be self-confident. Men are expected to pur-sue wealth or other accomplishments. If you do not, you will not be valued as high-

highly by many members of society, including many attractive women. So even if you weren't driven to "male" behaviors, you might adopt them anyway, because doing what society expects of you can make your life easier and better.

However, correlation does not imply causation. Some gender-based preferences are unquestionably innate. Even one-day-old infants – far too young to know or care what society wants them to do - adopt traditional gender roles. When shown both a mechanical mobile and a human face, boys' eyes tend to lock onto the mobile, while girls' eyes focus on the face. And at one year of age, when shown silent videos of a car running and of two people talking, boys disproportionately focused on the car, while girls were attracted to the conversation[1].

Thus, Magic Bullets starts from the premise that many human behavior patterns are innate. This is especially true for sexual decision-making, which is as important to evolutionary biology (or cultural identity, see below) as you can get. If we can understand women's fundamental impulses and motivations, then we can use these to our advantage in developing successful dating and relationship strategies. And if we can understand what women tend to have in common, then we will be more able to identify and interpret individual personality differences in areas where they do come into play.

One quick word about culture: Some cultural influences come from deep in the distant past, and have been inherited by most or all of the cultures that most readers of this book are likely to interact with. In the rest of this chapter, I refer primarily to evolutionary biology for simplicity's sake, but we can treat universal or near-universal cultural traits as having the same effect. They both drive human behavior in fundamental ways, whether we are conscious of them or not.

---

[1] *Simon Baron-Cohen, The Essential Difference. New York, Basic Books, 2003, pp. 2-6*

Quick primer on evolutionary biology

Darwin taught us how humans and other animals evolve. Animals in every generation have random genetic variation, and those animals whose genes are best suited for their environment tend to do a little better, on average, than other members of their species. Over time, the advantage of doing "a little better" becomes compounded, and the nature of the species changes.

Seen in this way, each generation is a competition between different genetic makeups. The competition takes place extremely slowly, but evolutionary time is very long. Assuming 30 years per generation, each million years[2] allows for over 33,000 rounds of Darwin's game.

Let's make a hypothetical example, starting with a world of 1,000 humans. Assume one of them was born with a mutation that the other 999 humans do not have: a dominant gene allowing him to eat trout. Most of the time, this ability would not be crucial, but on occasion trout-eating humans near freshwater lakes would be able to survive and reproduce while their non-trout-eating cousins would die of hunger[3]. If we assume that the ability to digest trout provided a 0.1% advantage on average to a given human's chances of surviving and raising healthy offspring, then, within one million years, 99.999999999.6% of the human population would be descended from this one person in one thousand who had the slightly superior gene. And the gene would now be part of normal human biology.

Much of our genetic makeup today is the result of random genetic mutations during previous generations. All other things being equal, a mutation that provides a genuine evolutionary advantage should win out over time.

What is an evolutionary advantage? Success, in evolutionary terms, can be seen as:

- Surviving until he or she is old enough to reproduce.

- Having access to mate(s) with whom to reproduce.

---

[2] *This is not to imply that humanity is one million years old; humanity is actually younger than that, but evolution is a continuous process and affected proto-humans in the same way that it affects "modern" humans.*

[3] *This may in fact be the first book written about meeting women that includes the phrase "non-trout-eating."*

- Having access to mate(s) with whom reproduction has a better-than-average chance of producing offspring who will themselves have greater chances of evolutionary success.

- Reproducing frequently (but not so frequently as to cause a burden).

- Being able to protect and raise their offspring to maximize their chances of success.

Looking at this list, it should become apparent why evolutionary biology is so important to the science of dating. Other than the basic need to survive, every component of evolutionary success relates directly to effectively choosing a mate and managing a relationship, which is why you are reading this book. Let's look at the consequences of unsuccessful mating and relationship strategies:

- If you do not have access to mate(s), your genes will die out in one generation.

- If you have access to mate(s) but are unable to conceive, your genes will die out in one generation.

- If you are able to conceive, but your children are unable to mate or conceive, your genes will die out in two generations.

- If you are able to conceive healthy and desirable offspring but you are unable to raise them and protect them, your genes will die out in two generations.

It took us 33,330 generations to get our ancestors to eat trout in our hypothetical example. It takes one or two generations to wipe out genes that are not optimally designed for sexual behavior. A harsh reality, but one that highlights the cost of failure and why sexual decision-making is so intensely driven by evolutionary-biological impulses.

Evolutionary biology today

Our biological makeup was primarily developed in the previous hundreds of thousands of years of pre-history (what I am going to call evolutionary time). However, our environment has changed extremely quickly over the past few thousand years, and evolution could not possibly have kept pace.

Today many of our biological influences are designed for an environment that no longer exists. For example, food was relatively scarce for most of evolutionary time. As fat is an efficient way to store energy on the body, humans who were predisposed to liking fat had an evolutionary advantage.

Thus, most people today have a taste for fatty foods, despite food not being scarce in most of the developed world.

Many of our strongest sexual preferences can be attributed to evolutionary development.

For example:

- People are generally not sexually attracted to close family members (increased chances of unhealthy offspring).

- Men have extreme emotional responses to female infidelity (nothing is worse, in evolutionary biological terms, than spending your time and resources to raise another man's offspring).

- People prefer to conceive their own children than to adopt.

- Men tend to prefer women with wide, rather than narrow, hips.

Let's use the last of these as an example. In the past, childbirth was risky and many mothers and children died. Women with wider hips had a better chance giving birth successfully, so men who were biologically predisposed to mate with such women tended to have more surviving children. They also had a greater chance of their wives surviving and contributing to the family. The evolutionary advantage was such that most men today tend to appreciate wider hips, even though today death in childbirth is rare, at least in the developed world.

Evolutionary biology for women

Just as men generally prefer wider hips, women have near-universal preferences as well. We can divide them into three categories:

Foundations:

> Health.
> Social Intuition.
> Humor.

Attributes:

> Status.
> Wealth.

Congruence:

> Pre-selected.
> Challenging.
> Confident.

Note that these are not the only or even the necessary characteristics to win a woman's interest. These are simply the most important qualities that are common to most women. Every woman will also have her unique interests when it comes to men, and most are also looking for elements which must be built together, like trust, connection, and shared values. Nevertheless, if you know very little about a specific woman - which will often be the case before you get to know her – these are your eight key attraction switches. They have attracted women for generations.

Foundations

The "foundation" characteristics are deeply linked to evolutionary biology. In fact, they predate the human race.

Health

All animals are biologically-driven to seek healthy mates. The human female is no exception. A healthy man can provide his family with food, shelter, and protection.

His children are likelier to be healthy as well, allowing them to have healthy children of their own, and also to protect and provide for their parents in old age.

In general, appearing healthy is more about avoiding things that can hurt you than it is about things that will help you. It is often a necessary, but not sufficient, condition to attract desirable women.

Implications

- I'm not going to take the easy way out and tell you to go to the gym. Well, I will, but you probably already know that having a toned and fit body helps attract women, and if you haven't started working out yet, I'm probably not going to change your mind.

- If you don't work out, there is still hope. While having a fit and toned body contributes to being good-looking and to appearing healthy, it is not necessary. As long as you avoid the appearance of any major health problems, being good-looking for men in today's society is actually more dependent on fashion and grooming (see Chapter 21: Fashion) than it is on what you look like naked.

- If you can, tell stories that involve participating in physical activity.

- Never talk about being sick, about being tired, or bring to her attention anything unhealthy about you. Don't be weird and hide it if you have a headache, but realize that it won't help you.

- Skin blemishes indicate ill health. It's actually fairly easy to cover up most obvious skin problems like acne. I recommend seeing a facialist if you can afford one. Failing that, go to a makeup store and ask a salesperson to help find some cover-up that works with your skin tone.

- A balding hairline also connotes ill health. If you're balding, go bald, which is at least a choice as opposed to a health issue, or regenerate your hair.

- If you have glasses, consider contacts. Some men look good in glasses; most don't.

- Most of these things are easy to do; there is no excuse for scuttling your chances over health issues.

Social Intuition

The ability to thrive in a social group is extremely important for animals who live in groups, such as humans. When Aristotle wrote that "man is a political animal" he wasn't writing about elections or public policy; he was referring to the polis: ancient Greek for city. Humans are designed to live and to thrive in groups. In fact, one of the strongest punishments in Aristotle's Athens (and other traditional societies) was ostracism – exile from the tribe.

In evolutionary time, a man who was not respected within his group hurt his family's chances of success. Other people in the group would be less likely to share information, resources, protection or opportunities with him.

Have you ever met a man who always seems to say or do the wrong thing? His manners are different, or he talks too much or about things which are of no interest or are inappropriate. Possibly, his general demeanor just doesn't feel "right." This guy probably doesn't do very well with women, because he doesn't have Social Intuition.

You can't instantly develop social skills. Social skills are the underlying theme of this book, and improving them will take work. So my advice here will be fairly foundational – none of it will get you more dates right off the bat, but these are important things to keep in mind as you read the rest of this book. For tips that you can use tonight, you should be reading Chapter 2 anyway.

Implications

- Social Intuition comes from repeated practice and observation. Make a conscious effort to interact with more people, especially people who have strong social skills themselves. Attend more social gatherings – anything from your college alumni's get-togethers to cocktail parties and happy hours. Practice, practice, practice, and observe what other people do in response to what you do.

- Waiters interact with people all day. Computer programmers generally don't. Which profession is better for developing social skills? No one is telling you to quit your job, but if you are in a low-social skills profession, you'll need to make a conscious effort to interact socially with people who do have social intuition.

- TV and movies are not real life. This sounds obvious, but it's not. People learn about patterns of behavior from observation. You can't help but internalize behavior patterns you see on the screen. Make a conscious effort to avoid this. Don't try to act like a movie or TV character. Better still, spend more time interacting with people and less time interacting with your television.

- For professional training, you can take a Love Systems' workshop (See Chapter 24 for more professional resources). While the focus of our workshops is in teaching, demonstrating and using various tools to help you succeed with women, these workshops are also highly personalized. If we notice issues relating to social intuition, we will tell you and we will help you overcome them.

Humor

You might be surprised to see humor in a list of foundational evolutionary characteristics. Humor is often considered to be based on language, which would make it culturally-specific and not universal.

However, recent research has disproved this. Humor not only pre-dates language and exists in every culture on the planet, but it is also present in other animals, such as monkeys, dogs, and rats. No, rats don't actually laugh, but they do make a specific high-pitched vocalization when tickled or at play.

Having a sense of humor means you can share laughter and induce it in others. This may seem frivolous, but it's not. According to one expert, "most laughter is not about humor; it is about relationships between people." Laughter is a communication tool. Chimps laugh when they play-fight, to communicate that they are playing, not attacking. More importantly for our purposes, laughter creates social bonds between people who share it. When you laugh with someone, you feel a closer tie to them. The very act of laughing releases chemicals in your body that trigger positive emotions. Thus, people are predisposed to enjoy laughter and people who can make them laugh.

As a communication and social tool, humor could be considered to be part of Social Intuition, but it gets a section of its own because it is so important. The importance we place on humor should come as no surprise. Whereas many women will deny or not even realize that factors such as wealth or pre-selection affect their preferences in men, most will say that a sense of humor is extremely important. And they're right.

Implications

- Humor can be learned like any other social skill. If you don't have a good sense of humor, develop one. We polled members of The Attraction Forums (the leading free dating science community in the world) – specifically those men who had sought out to improve their sense of humor – and these are some of the resources they recommended:

    Humor Theory: Formula of Laughter by Igor Krichtafovitch

    Only Joking by Jimmy Carr

    True and False: Heresy and Common Sense for the Actor by David Mamet

    Three Uses of the Knife by David Mamet

    Comedian (movie) by Jerry Seinfeld

- Make a point of observing people who have a good sense of humor. Don't just focus on what someone says; much more important is the associated timing, tonality, and delivery. Go to comedy clubs to observe professionals.

- Don't fall into the trap of turning into a clown. You can get cheap laughs by doing weird or inappropriate things, but that makes people laugh at you instead of with you. It's good to be able to laugh at yourself (see below), but don't deliberately lower your social status.

- Don't take yourself too seriously. A self-deprecating wit, used in moderation, can actually convey high status and high value. If someone makes a friendly joke at your expense that others are also laughing at, laugh with them.

- There are many types of humor: sarcastic humor, slapstick humor, satirical humor, etc. Make sure your sense of humor is wide-ranging. The same type of humor over and over can be grating.

- Laughter is contagious. Even if you're not producing all the humor, being able to find and laugh at other funny things that are going on will encourage others to laugh as well. This catalyzes good emotions and social bonding.

Summary

Now that we've finished the foundations section, let's review what we have. In evolutionary terms, a man who has health, social intuition, and humor will also have the following qualities:

- His chances of continued survival are good.

- He can likely produce healthy children.

- He can participate and thrive in different social groups.

- He can make a woman feel good and make people feel close to him.

Is that enough to capture and keep the attention of a desirable woman? Not usually. But without them do you have a chance? Almost certainly not.

Attributes

If the foundational characteristics give you a "ticket to play" to win the interest of a desirable woman, your attributes give you a "ticket to win." Your attributes can be thought of as something external to you (as opposed to something thought of as intrinsic, like health) and relate to something you have, as opposed to something you are.

From an evolutionary standpoint, pretty much everything external that consistently attracts women can be related either to status or to wealth. This doesn't make women "golddiggers," though it helps explain why golddiggers exist. As we'll discuss below, women have good reasons to value these attributes in men.

Status

Status is associated with power. Power implies the ability to cause things to happen, or not happen. The strongest manifestation of power is the ability to help or hurt others. In evolutionary times, the chief had power and status. So did the medicine man. So did the religious authority. It is not difficult to see the evolutionary benefits of power. Today, politicians, CEOs, and movie producers are examples of people who have power and status. Indeed, it is not uncommon to see such men involved with sexually desirable women whom they would not have otherwise been likely to attract.

Power can also be applied indirectly. The chief's trusted advisors carry power through their ability to influence the chief. The religious authority carries power through its ability to influence the supernatural. Being close to a high-status person carries status in itself.

Of course, status is attractive for non-evolutionary reasons as well. All other things being equal, being with a high-status man allows a woman to lead a more interesting and exciting life than if she were paired with a low-status man.

Status exists in a relative context. A university professor won't likely have much status at a fashion show because many models don't know or care much about academia, and academic status is not particularly relevant to most of their lives. He would have much more status at a book club or dinner party where more women would likely find higher education to be more relevant to their own experience. Similarly, a movie producer would have little relevant status to a woman who doesn't care about the entertainment industry, though she might still be attracted to his wealth, ambition, or other factors. However, to many young women, being a movie producer is one of the most powerful identities one could possess. The higher-status a woman, the more she will desire an equal or higher-status man.

This relative context can be very narrow. Many women sleep with their bosses. This is sometimes to advance or avoid negative consequences to their career, but is often genuinely consensual and based in part on a woman's attraction to her boss' relative power and status. Even if the manager of a small restaurant has little power and status outside his restaurant, he has a lot inside, and this can be attractive to the women who work for him.

Power has its greatest impact when its holder is willing to exercise it. If I own a nightclub, but it's the doorman who decides who gets inside and who gets into the VIP room, then he has more power than I do until I exercise my power. On the other hand, many women tend to be cautious of men who exercise their power indiscriminately, or in a way that might cause them danger. Think James Caan (Sonny) in The Godfather. However, one place where women expect men to exercise power – in a judicious way - is in protecting those around them. She will want to know you can protect her too. Don't hit on this theme over and over, but a reference or two can help you. This is what some of us used to call being the "Protector of Loved Ones."

Implications

- Relative status is far easier to obtain than absolute status. If you go to a restaurant frequently, get to know everyone who works there. Even if no one knows you outside the door, you can be a celebrity inside. Plan your social events to become well-known at a few venues rather than a stranger at many. Take advantage of this on dates (Chapter 16).

- Status is often demonstrated relative to other men. Recognize and seek opportunities to display status in a non-confrontational way over other men, such as teaching another man something or expressing dominant body language (see Chapter 18: Body Language).

- Act like people expect high-status men to act. Such men do not tend to be envious. They do not tend to denigrate the success of others, particularly other high-status men. They do not tend to be needy, to go out of their way to convince others of their status, or to worry about what others think of them. And so on.

Wealth

Wealth means having access to resources. In evolutionary time, "wealth" might refer to a man's hidden store of food and animal pelts. Today, it's money.

Financial security is crucial to evolutionary success. Men are predisposed to accumulate wealth, even when they already have plenty. Both men and women desire financial security and our emotions make us uncomfortable when we do not have it. Women especially have an emotional need to know that they will have access to sufficient resources for themselves and their children to thrive.

While women are able to create their own wealth in today's society, most women retain an evolutionary desire for a man who could provide for her and future children. This doesn't mean that most women necessarily expect a man to provide for her; they just want a man's income to be at a level where he could. Being on the road to wealth is almost the same as having it; most women will consider a medical student's prospects to be almost as good as a doctor's. Even some of my most liberal and feminist female friends feel uncomfortable with men who make less money than they do, or worry that a man in this position would feel emasculated and resentful. Put simply, whether based on culture or biology, women are predisposed to be attracted to men with money who can provide a comfortable lifestyle.

No one likes to move to a lower socio-economic level, so a woman accustomed to a certain lifestyle will set expectations accordingly. Don't think of this as a moral issue. Valuing a man's wallet is no more "shallow" than valuing a woman's chest. If you've dated beauty queens your whole life, it would take a lot more for the "girl next door" to impress you than if you'd dated average-looking women.

Wealth has diminishing returns for most women once you reach their comfort threshold. Some women are strongly attracted to wealth above this level and can be interested in a man based primarily on his wealth. These women are sometimes called "golddiggers." Golddiggers view their sexuality in part as a tool to "move up" in society. In evolutionary time, and in many societies today, marrying well is one of the few ways realistically open for women to improve their status and lifestyle. If this bothers you, then don't date these women. They are easy to spot. If you're trying to act like a high-status man, you should act as though the existence of such women is nothing new to you.

Implications

- Men have been trying to tempt women with wealth since evolutionary time. Don't be sleazy. Displays of wealth should be subtle and appear natural. If you take your wallet out to buy a drink and it happens to be full of $100 bills, that's subtle and natural. If you reach into your pocket and pull out your tax return, it isn't.

- Some displays of wealth – like some expensive cars, especially smaller sports cars – can be considered as "compensating" and can be a big turnoff for some women.

- Women look for consistency with wealth. A man at a VIP table who dresses badly and drives a cheap car is not usually seen as a man with wealth; he's seen as a man with a spending problem.

- Don't worry if you're not rich. Just don't look like you are struggling. Don't talk about financial difficulties or borrowing money, and don't make a big deal out of expenses. Make sure your car is clean and in good repair – not doing so is a very obvious indicator of wealth or lifestyle difficulties.

- Use your money wisely. If you have $110 in your wallet, wrap a $100 bill around ten $1s instead of having eleven $10 bills. Spending an extra $20 on a coat won't make much of a difference, but spending an extra $20 on wine will.

- If you don't have wealth, the next best thing is to show that you have the potential for it. Show that you are ambitious and have a plan.

Summary

- By displaying the two key attributes of status and wealth, a man communicates to women that he:

  1.) Lives an exciting lifestyle that she can share.
  2.) Can provide for himself, his wife, and his children in comfort.

- In addition to this, if you've already covered the foundations – health, social intuition, and humor – you've covered most of the bases from an evolutionary standpoint. This does not mean that you'll attract every woman. People are individuals with their own idiosyncrasies and frequently make choices that go against their evolutionary programming. This is a key factor that separates humans from other animals. And you still have competition from other men who can also demonstrate these qualities. But you'll still have the important bases covered.

- Remember though that you not only have to have and display these qualities, you have to be congruent with them.

Congruence

In this context, congruence refers to having an internally consistent personality.

Attractive women meet, literally, thousands of men who show at least some interest in them. Many of these men will exaggerate or invent things about themselves to attract her. Women learn very quickly not to take what a man says at face value if they think he is trying to win her interest.

Women look for congruence. If a man supposedly has wealth and status, most women would expect him to act accordingly. He should be confident, pre-selected by other women, and a challenge.

These qualities are important because women need to be able to make quick judgments about men and assess their credibility. Many women place a lot of importance on the "congruence qualities" discussed in this section, as a man is less likely to convincingly fake these than he is to successfully lie about having wealth and status. Women have to do this. Otherwise they will waste their time dating supposed movie moguls who actually don't have a job.

Consider a man who implied that he was an Olympic athlete, had friends who were movie stars, used to work as a professional comedian, and owns a mansion in Beverly Hills. Most women would probably be impressed. But if he was also shifty-eyed, made nervous gestures, seemed terrified of women, and jumped at any opportunity for a date that crossed his path, most women would be turned off. He would simply not be congruent.

A lot of the time that women want to wait before getting physical with a man is based on congruence-checking. If a man "seems" great when she first meets him, the next date or two is often her time to assess whether he really is that person. (Don't worry; we have a system for compressing or bypassing this process.)

In fact, congruence is so important that women often undertake this process in reverse. They know that men who are confident, pre-selected, and challenging will usually have lots going for them, and men who are not, generally do not. So many women will start out by looking for men who display the congruent qualities of being confident, pre-selected, and challenging.

Confidence

Remember when you were nervous the first time you drove a car? You didn't really know what to do, you didn't think your chances of success without someone helping you would be very good, and you drove slowly and tentatively. You hoped nothing unusual or threatening would happen because you knew you might not be able to handle it.

But then you got good at driving. You know you're good at it. It's no big deal. You can do it while listening to the radio, eating a sandwich, or talking to passengers. You can have fun. You can handle more or less anything that's likely to happen on the road.

Now think about confidence in general. A man who is confident is essentially saying to himself: "I'm good at this stuff. I can handle more or less anything that's likely to happen to me here. And I can have fun doing it." Unless he's delusional, this confidence probably comes from having been successful. So a woman sees a confident man, and she feels good around him. She assumes he knows what he's doing, that things are no big deal and he can have fun, and he can handle whatever life might throw at him.

Incidentally, this is one reason why things like body language (see Chapter 19) are so important. Let's take relaxed shoulders as an example, which is just one of dozens of elements of confident body language. There's nothing inherently attractive about relaxed shoulders. Look at yourself in the mirror. Relax your shoulders and let them fall back. Now tighten them and raise them. Do you think you look any sexier or less sexy? Probably not.

However, confident men are disproportionately likely to spend more time with their shoulders relaxed. Because they are confident, they can do this. They don't have to be on edge all the time, always vigilant for threats. They are secure in their position and their skills. (They'd better be, or their confidence will be their downfall...)

Over time, women who like men with relaxed shoulders tend to end up with a greater share of confident men. And if confidence is correlated with success, then this means that they end up with a greater share of successful men. That means their children will be more successful. Over time, their children will overwhelm the children of women who mate with men with tense shoulders. Even though there's nothing inherently sexy about relaxed shoulders, or eye contact, or standing with your feet a decent distance apart, or any physical indicator of confidence, these little things add up to make all the difference in the world.

In any case, it's probably not news to you that confidence is sexually attractive to women. So let's move into some of the implications.

Implications

- Men tend to develop confidence by increasing achievement with things that can be measured. Working out not only helps your Health (see above), but as you improve from a 100lb bench press to a 110lb bench press and from a 10-minute to a 9-minute mile, it develops a feeling of accomplishment that can influence other areas of your life.

- Keep a journal or a private blog – and make it simple so it doesn't become a burden. You'll be surprised at how much success you will enjoy using the techniques from Magic Bullets. Break your social life down into steps. Did you successfully approach any beautiful women today? Are you better at it than last week? How many dates did you have last month? Compare that to how many dates you'll have in this coming month. Men who study dating science often aren't aware of the progress they've been making unless they keep detailed notes. It's very easy to despair at the road ahead of you if you don't keep an eye on the distance you've already covered.

- Consciously base your self-esteem on factors other than women's approval.

- Don't be arrogant. People who talk about how great they are all the time (even though they are genuinely very good at a specific thing) are generally thought by others to be deeply insecure. Insecurity reflects a lack of self-confidence. People will eventually clue into that, and you'll have difficulty actually keeping a girlfriend. If you're that person, and you don't change, you'll likely end up alone, surrounded by people who think they can get something out of you or who are just as insecure as you.

Pre-selection

Women know – and their biological impulses certainly know – that whether other women are attracted to a man is a useful guide for them. While individual tastes differ, most women know that they are looking for roughly the same qualities as the rest of their gender: health, confidence, status, and so on. When women are interested in you, you are pre-selected and therefore more interesting to other women.

In contrast, the absence of pre-selection can put a man at a disadvantage. If a woman infers that other women are not interested in someone, she has only three likely explanations. Her tastes could be dramatically different from the rest of her gender. She possesses unusual insight and is better at determining a man's true nature than other women. Or other women are not interested in him for a reason.

Usually men who are rejected by large numbers of women are undesirable (or, in our terms, evolutionarily disadvantaged) in some way. Thus, women who buck the trend and mate with unpopular men do not tend to pass on their genes very well.

On the other hand, pre-selection is best displayed in moderation. Let's assume a man is irresistible.

Women then may question whether such a man would stay with her. Remember, a process like pre-selection which is driven by evolutionary biology exists because of its evolutionary result: the creation of successful offspring. Unless she has some reason to think, or deludes herself into thinking, that he will stay with her and help raise their children, she might not have sex with him and pre-selection won't help him. A pregnant woman with no one to protect her or provide for her and her child has significantly reduced evolutionary prospects.

Implications

- Never talk about lack of success with women or "open up" to her by revealing something like how your ex-girlfriend dumped you or how lonely you are. This remains true even if a woman has just told you something similar about herself. But don't make the opposite mistake either.

- Pre-selection should be communicated subtly. If you are enjoying increased success with women compared to the past, it is natural to want to talk about this. Don't.

- Ambiguity is your friend. Being seen with or referring to attractive female "friends" is great. You won't necessarily come across as a player, but a woman will realize that other women are intrigued by you.

- Pre-selection is contextual and relative. A woman will be most affected by pre-selection from other women whose opinion she trusts, who are most like her, or who are at or above her level. The concept of a woman's social value is explained in Chapter 7 (Attraction).

Challenging

A man who is successful in life will generally want to be with a desirable woman. He won't rush at the first woman he sees, he'll have standards, and he won't be easy to win over. In short, he's a challenge.

People value what they have to work for. If you go through a series of grueling interviews with a company before they give you a job, you'll feel differently about it than if they offered it to you after a five minute interview. People like to be internally consistent. So if you believe that it was worth going through those interviews, you will want to believe that the job you got was worth it. Otherwise, you would have to wonder why you went through that experience.

Some initiation rituals in college fraternities in the United States have a similar purpose. These rituals can be purposefully unpleasant and intense. If you complete them, you will be psychologically predisposed to believing that the rituals were "worth it" because being part of the fraternity is such a positive experience. [I have no opinion on this one way or another; fraternities were not a big part of campus life at my college.]

Implications

- Never give off the impression that you are desperate or lonely.

- Make her work to get you. Not too much, or she'll get bored or frustrated, but ensure that there is some doubt in her mind before you commit. This is one of the major processes that takes places in Qualification (Chapter 8).

- Just because she is interested in you is NOT a reason for you to be interested in her. This is also part of Qualification.

- Don't play too hard to get either. Especially before she's had a chance to get really into you, playing aloof won't interest her.

- Don't be affected by the little games some women play.

With these three congruent qualities we now have a strong evolutionary profile. A man who was able to display all of the above characteristics would be:

- Healthy.

- Socially Skilled (Social Intuition).

- Funny (Humor).

- High-status.

- Wealthy.

- Confident.

- Pre-selected.

- Challenging.

I would wager that if you were to show this list to your single female friends, most of them would want to meet such a man. For you to be that man, we still have some work to do. First, you need to be able to present these qualities to women who you don't know in large social gatherings where there are lots of distractions and other pitfalls. This is the primary goal of the first three phases of the Emotional Progression Model, from Opening to Attraction, and also plays a role in Qualification. Second, you need to build a connection with a woman based on more than biology – to recognize and engage her uniqueness and to advance your interaction toward a sexual relationship and beyond. This is the main goal of the last four phases of the Model, from Qualification to Relationship.

4

IN THIS CHAPTER

- Emotions and Sexual Behavior

- Emotional Triggers

- A Comprehensive Model

- Insights

- Emotional Momentum

Introduction

You see an attractive woman at a restaurant. Or maybe you're introduced to her at a party. What do you do now?

If you're like most men, you don't have a plan beyond "get to know her" or "start talking to her and see what happens." But as for what you actually do, the possibilities are endless. Do you:

- Say hi?

- Ask her name?

- Ask a question?

- Tell her a story?

- Deliver your best "pickup line?"

There are literally billions upon billions of possible things you could be doing, especially when you take your body language and tonality into account. Your actions will combine with her personality and mood to create a particular emotional impression. She will react and then it's your turn again, with another set of infinite choices based on the new situation. There are so many possibilities and variables involved that the world's most powerful computers would not be able to model even the first half-second of your interaction.

This is part of the reason why meeting women can be stressful and frustrating for men. Our brains are configured to break down a big process into a series of smaller, logically-connected tasks. Say you're setting up a campsite with some friends. Your overall goal is to survive the night in some comfort.

You know that to do this you need to build a tent, start a fire, and so on. And for each objective, you can learn the steps required to make it happen. Most men are intellectually comfortable in this sort of situation.

Succeeding with women is more complicated because meeting women is an interactive process, and people's personalities are unique, complex, and variable. In contrast, your campsite doesn't care how you build a fire. You don't have to be subtle or worry about embarrassing it in front of its friends.

Matches don't go in and out of emotional states where they sometimes want to be lit and sometimes they want to go home.

Fortunately, we don't have to throw up our hands in frustration. Human behavior will never be as predictable as building a fire, but through intelligent hypothesis-generation, an amazing amount of testing, and a good dose of humility about the limitations and applicability of any individual insight, we can identify productive paths to succeeding with women.

Emotions and Sexual Behavior

Most women tend to make sexual decisions based more on their emotional state than pure physical attraction. This does not mean that your looks are not important. They absolutely are, and if you are good-looking, some women will have sex with you based on your looks alone. However, while women vary greatly, most of the time you will need to make an emotional impact. One thing we've found in our combined tens of thousands of approaches is that there are four emotional triggers that – if you can activate them all – tend to make women say yes.

These are:

> Feeling that a man's value is equal to or greater than hers.

> Feeling that she's special to him or that she's earned his attention.

> Feeling comfort and connection with him.

> Feeling aroused by his touch without awkwardness or embarrassment.

In general, your best chance of sleeping with a woman is to trigger these four emotions in her.

Emotional Triggers

Let's briefly look at these triggers to help develop a model for female sexual behavior.

> Feeling that a man's value is equal to or greater than hers.

The concept of value is explained in Chapter 7. Essentially, women like to sleep with men who are "better" than them. This is what creates attraction in a woman and explains why we call the time when we are trying to create this emotion in her the Attraction phase (Chapter 7: Attraction).

Feeling that she's special to him or that she's earned his attention.

Most women like to feel that they have earned a man's attention and that he is interested in her for more than her looks. They like to feel "qualified," so we call this the Qualification phase. Qualification is where you make your interest in her explicit. You should not show signs of interest in her until she has shown signs of interest in you, which usually happens in Attraction.

Feeling comfort and connection with him.

We call this the Comfort phase, which is the longest in the Emotional Progression Model.

It begins toward the end of the Qualification phase, when it's clear that both of you are interested in each other. It ends when you have established enough comfort and connection with her that she is comfortable being in a sexual situation with you. A sexual situation is one in which a woman is engaging in sexual behavior (touching that goes beyond kissing) in a place where sex could realistically happen.

Feeling aroused by his touch without awkwardness or embarrassment.

We call this the Seduction phase. Seduction is the only phase in the Emotional Progression Model that can really be measured physically. The closer you are (physically) to sex, the further along you are in the phase. Seduction is primarily based on intensifying her willingness to have sex with you and mitigating her reasons not to. Once you have sex, the Seduction phase is over.

Thus these four triggers form the backbone of the Emotional Progression Model. And they generally come in this order:

Attraction (Chapter 7).

Qualification (Chapter 8).

Comfort (Chapter 9).

Seduction (Chapter 10).

In fact, these are the only four phases you may need if you are introduced to someone through your Social Circle (Chapter 12) and all you're looking for is a one-night stand.

A Comprehensive Model

Of course, much of the time you are going to want to meet women who aren't already in your social circle. Whether you see a woman at a nightclub or a bookstore, you need the tools to approach her and start a conversation. We call this the Approaching phase:

Approaching: Starting a single-subject conversation with someone.

Approaching focuses on approaching a woman you don't know (or more often approaching her and whatever group of people she is with, since women tend not to go to social events alone) and starting a conversation.

That still leaves a hole in the development of conversation. It's not natural to jump from approaching a group of strangers to spending time with them and conveying value (the Attraction phase). This helped us identify the necessity for the Transitioning phase:

Transitioning: Turning a single-subject approach into a normal, free-flowing conversation.

Transitioning turns a simple interaction into a longer conversation by introducing at least one new topic and changing the dynamic of your interaction. This is an important phase – and one newly formalized for this book – that turns approaches into conversations.

With Approaching and Transitioning and the four emotionally-based phases addressed previously, we have a path from meeting a stranger to beginning a sexual relationship with her. Another innovation in this book is that we take the process one step further, with the Relationship phase:

Relationship: Managing the subsequent relationship.

After the Seduction phase, you've got the whole "what next?" question to deal with. Do you want her as your girlfriend? Someone to date? A friend with benefits? The Relationship phase takes you through this, and how to sustain and develop the type of relationship you want.

Adding these three phases creates the full Emotional Progression Model:

The Emotional Progression Model

1. Approaching (Chapter 5)

2. Transitioning (Chapter 6)

3. Attraction (Chapter 7)

4. Qualification (Chapter 8)

5. Comfort (Chapter 9)

6. Seduction (Chapter 10)

Insights

The stages of the model function as intermediate goals and measures of your progress. It's not a strictly linear process – Attraction overlaps a bit into Qualification, both Attraction and Qualification bleed into Comfort, and the Relationship phase done properly starts in Comfort as well – but the phases are essentially sequential.

The general overall linearity of the Emotional Progression Model yields five big insights:

1. Attraction comes before Qualification.

    • Make a woman attracted to you before showing significant interest in her.

2. Attraction comes before Comfort.

    • Make a woman attracted to you before looking for commonalities, deep conversations, etc.

3. Qualification comes before Comfort

- Have a woman work to win your interest before you open up to each other.

4. Comfort comes before Seduction

- Help a woman feel connected to you before progressing sexually.

5. Seduction comes before Relationships

- Whatever you want with a woman, your medium-term goal is to sleep with her.

The last of these might been surprising – and has certainly been controversial. A common insight into female sexual behavior is that women will often delay sex for some time with a man she sees as a potential boyfriend while satisfying physical needs with another man or other men in the meantime.

While this is true, it does not mean that the man who is "dating and waiting" has the best chance of becoming her boyfriend. Very little builds as much intimacy with a woman as repeated sexual encounters. Sleep with her first, and then concentrate on showing her you'd be a good boyfriend rather than showing her you'd be a good boyfriend and then trying to sleep with her.

Emotional Momentum

A further insight concerns the principle of emotional momentum. Emotional momentum explains why most interactions need to move forward or die. You can't stay in any particular phase forever. It will bore or frustrate most women. Even within a phase, you need to be moving forward. Say you had a great three hours meeting a woman at a party and made it all the way to the Comfort phase, but the next two weeks consisted of both of you unluckily leaving messages on each other's voicemail.

You will likely lose emotional momentum and your chances with her. Emotional momentum can work against you through no fault of your own.

Emotional momentum can also work for you. Each phase that you can smoothly pass through builds up your momentum for the next one. When a woman talks about sleeping with you and says "it just happened," that's emotional momentum at work (and good Seduction skills). The whole process should happen quickly, not over months.

So that's a quick overview of the Emotional Progression Model. Now let's go into some more detail and get to the nuts and bolts of how to use it.

5

IN THIS CHAPTER

What is Approaching?

It's not normal to start conversations with strangers. It can even be intimidating. However, everything that follows in Magic Bullets is based on you being able to approach attractive women without awkwardness and smoothly start a conversation. We call this process "Approaching" and the ways we start conversations "Openers."

You might be wondering why you need to have specific ways to start talking to someone. Can't you just walk up to a woman and say "Hi, I'm Joe" and start a conversation? Yes, you can, and it might even work. We discuss this type of opener later in this chapter in the section entitled "No Opener." In general, however, we find that most attractive women are hit on so often by so many different men.

"Success," in the context of opening, means getting to a normal conversation with a woman. A normal conversation is one that can range freely over a variety of topics, including personal ones. As you will see, some openers will get you all the way to a normal conversation, while others will require a Transition (Chapter 6). Neither approach is inherently better than the other, and we routinely use both.

When you approach, you usually start a conversation about one specific topic. Getting to your Transition or to a normal conversation should take anywhere from ten seconds to two minutes. If you take much longer, both the single topic and the interaction as a whole risks becoming stale and it can become awkward to transition to other topics and develop the conversation.

Throughout this chapter – indeed, throughout the Emotional Progression Model – we talk about meeting women. However, women do not tend to be alone in social situations. So when we talk about approaching a woman, we usually mean approaching her group. In the Approaching phase, engage the entire group and don't pay particular attention to the woman in whom you are interested.

By the way, if you are introduced to a woman through someone you already know, you can usually assume that you have the freedom to have a normal conversation. We call these sorts of introductions "meeting through your Social Circle" (see Chapter 12 for more details). In these situations, you don't really need to use the opening techniques from this chapter (or the Transitioning techniques from the following chapter); you can skip straight to the Attraction phase (Chapter 7).

What follows are six broad types of openers and a discussion of non-verbal elements in opening. In general, it's your non-verbal elements that will make your opener succeed or fail, so if you're new to this sort of material, I'd pick an easy kind of opener to begin with (such as opinion openers) and then focus heavily on the non-verbal elements.

Types of openers

You can classify openers along a risk-reward continuum. A low risk-reward opener is more likely to get a woman to respond (requires less compliance), but is less likely to lead to a normal conversation. For example, if you ask a woman for the time, the social rules of modern society more or less require her to answer. However, it can be awkward to move from discussing the time (the opener) to discussing subjects that can engage her emotionally (a normal conversation). This makes asking for the time a generally poor choice of opener. Many low risk-reward openers tend to focus on topics that do not relate to you or her.

In contrast, high risk-reward openers tend to be unequivocally about the two of you. The risk is that you will not successfully open – that is to say, that she will not want to talk to you. The potential reward is that you will move forward much quicker to a normal conversation. For example, you can open with: "Why don't we go sit over there and get to know each other?" Most desirable women would say no to such an approach from a stranger – but if the answer is yes, you will already be in a normal conversation. We will discuss better high risk-reward openers toward the end of this chapter.

There are six major types of openers. We will look at these in order of their risk-reward profiles, from the lowest to the highest:

The Opener Risk/Reward Continuum					
Functional	Opinion	Situational	No Opener	Screening	Direct

Functional Openers

The Opener Risk/Reward Continuum					
Functional	Opinion	Situational	No Opener	Screening	Direct

Functional openers carry the lowest risk-reward profile. They relate to conversational subjects (usually questions) that most people feel socially obligated to answer. For example: "Do you have a light?" or "Do you know how to get to X Street / X Restaurant / X Place?"

It is quite possible to use these and succeed, especially if you are approaching a woman who is alone and there is very little else to distract her attention (waiting in line, on an airplane, etc.). For this reason, functional openers are most often used in Day Game (Chapter 13). See the "A successful functional opener" sidebar on the following page.

The trouble with functional openers is that they can make Transitioning difficult. Men who have success with Functional openers usually plan to move directly to another type of opener immediately afterward; they're difficult to succeed with on their own. However, if you are too shy to start conversations with women you don't know, you can start building up your confidence (and enjoy the occasional success) with them.

Opinion Openers

The Opener Risk/Reward Continuum					
Functional	Opinion	Situational	No Opener	Screening	Direct

An opinion opener is exactly what it sounds like. You ask someone's opinion about something. For example:

- My friend Eddie over there in the green shirt just broke up with his girlfriend. How long do you think he has to wait before dating her friend?

- I'm planning my friend's birthday party next Friday and I'm trying to decide between an 80s theme and a jungle theme. What do you think?

- My friend keeps getting anonymous emails from a secret admirer but he thinks he knows who it is. Should he say something?

Do not use these! I literally made them up in the last five minutes. They came from my imagination, not your life. Why use an opener that others might be using and risk getting "caught" using a "pickup line?" Especially when there is no point – you will come across as a lot more genuine and in the moment if your opinion openers have genuine relevance to your life.

Start by thinking of a subject with broad interest that has happened to you or someone you know, and ask for an opinion on it. Good subjects for opinion openers are ones that generate emotional involvement, such as:

- Dating and relationships (but not about you)

- Gender differences or male-female issues

- Friendships

- Music and popular culture

Opinion openers should not have an obvious answer. If the opener can be answered with a simple "yes" or "no" (such as the "secret admirer" example above), ensure that the topic has sufficient depth that anyone answering the question would naturally want to explain their answer. The content of their answer or the explanation is usually irrelevant; the point is to start a conversation that interests her.

Opinion openers should also be neutral. This means that the opener does not imply that you like or dislike the people you are talking to, nor is your question obviously designed to get them to like or dislike you. Neutrality is important because you want to avoid her consciously having to decide whether she is attracted to you so early in your interaction.

Delaying a woman's decision can be important. As soon as a man says or does anything that a woman associates with being hit on, she needs to make a yes/no decision about whether she is curious about him. She has to. A desirable woman is approached so often that spending time getting to know every well-meaning man who starts talking to her would mean that she would have no time for herself.

Much of Part IV of this book ("Skills") will help you project yourself immediately as a man who most attractive women would be curious about. Opinion openers further increase your chances by delaying her decision about whether she is interested in you for a couple of minutes to give you that time to convey attractive qualities of your personality.

An opinion opener – unlike some of the higher risk-reward openers covered later in this chapter – will not generally help you in and of itself. Its primary purpose is to buy time. As such, you want to get through the opener and through the next phase (Transitioning) as quickly as possible, so you can get into the Attraction phase.

A Successful Functional Opener

It is possible to succeed with a functional opener. The following is an edited version of a field report by Harlequin, a member of The Attraction Forums, in February 2006. I've given the woman the arbitrary name of Julia and inserted Harlequin's commentary into square brackets [like this]. It's not necessarily an example of an ideal interaction, but it shows a functional opener that worked, and that's the point. The full post can be found at:

www.TheAttractionForums.com/forum/ showthread.php?t=5334

Harlequin: "Excuse me, do you have the time?" Julia: "2:20..."

Harlequin: "Damn, I'm late... do you know the

way to the sports centre? I got a game starting in 10 minutes..."

[She either knows or she doesn't...]

Harlequin: "It's just over there, huh? Damn what a trek... can I get a piggy back?"

[I was on the way to Leeds Olympic Pool – which had to be renamed Leeds International Pool because the builders messed up and made it one inch short of 50 meters. I was full of energy and enthusiasm and saw this woman. I approached her less than 500 yards from the pool and asked her for directions and she didn't know... so I teased her about this and then directed her to the pool. It was zany, but she loved it. Before I approached her, she was standing alone at the bus stop and then some nutter (me) approaches and makes her laugh. That made her happy that I was there; it's better than being alone. She ended up ignoring her bus when it came by.]

Harlequin: "What? That was yours? You just missed your bus?"

Julia: "Yeah... I'm supposed to signal"

Harlequin: "Wow... not only do you not know where the world's greatest non-Olympic pool is, but you suck with public transport..."

Julia: "Well I was kind of distracted..."

Harlequin: "Are you one of those women that stands on the street at night... waiting for taxis, or are you the sort that books one in advance?"

...and off Harlequin and Julia go into a normal conversation.

Opinion openers often turn into scripts as you get used to the likely range of responses and develop natural follow-on questions. You want to end the opener and get to the Transitioning phase as quickly as possible, but sometimes you need an extra moment or two of dialogue before the moment is right. In these situations, use follow-on statements or questions. See the "Breast Enlargement" sidebar on the following page as an example.

There are three other important elements that improve any opinion opener:

1. ■ **Time Constraints:** Somewhere in the first 30 seconds you should say something like "I can only stay a second; I have my friends here." This will stop the group from feeling uncomfortable and wondering how long you'll be staying. A time constraint implies that you are not hitting on anyone and also sets you up as a bit of a challenge. But make sure you phrase your time constraint in positive terms. For example, consider the difference in what is communicated by "I can only stay a second; my friends are here" compared to "I will only stay a second, then I'll stop bothering you."

2. ■ **Rooting:** If a woman does not believe that your opinion opener reflects a real situation that is relevant to you, then she may think you are hitting on her in an amateurish way. Adding specific details to the opener to make the situation feel more real to her is known as rooting. Consider the difference between "My friend Eddie over there in the green shirt just broke up with his girlfriend. How long do you think he has to wait before dating her friend?" and "How long should someone wait after breaking up with their girlfriend to date her friend?" The rooting of the former opener in specific details gives it credibility. If a woman responds to an opinion opener with something like "are you taking a survey?" it often means you did not convincingly root your question.

3. ■ **Attention... Pause:** Opinion openers are usually longer than other types of openers, so make sure you have a group's full attention before you start. We have found opening with "hey guys" in a loud tone of voice to be successful at getting a group's attention. Pause after you say this. If the group does not stop their conversation to look at you, repeat yourself, a bit louder. If you routinely need a second attempt to get their attention, you are not being loud and authoritative enough. By the way, we use "guys" instead of "girls" or "ladies" even when addressing an all-female group, because using a gender-neutral term ["guys" can be gender-neutral at least in North America] implies that it is irrelevant that they are women, which further implies that you are not hitting on them.

We love opinion openers. Their ability to start a conversation without communicating interest is invaluable, especially when meeting very attractive women. They can also reduce approach anxiety (see the end of this chapter) because they are scripted and neutral. Because they are scripted, they are also great for practicing and improving your tonality and your non-verbal communication, since you already know what you're going to say.

On the other hand, opinion openers have some disadvantages. They tend to be longer, which makes them harder to use in loud nightclubs. You will also need a good transition to move from the specific subject of the opener to a normal conversation.

An opinion opener must appear to be spontaneous to be successful. If you walk across a room to ask a woman's opinion, she'll know that you picked her for a reason and she will start screening you. If you want to use an opinion opener on her, you will need to first maneuver yourself to an adjacent space before "spontaneously" turning to her and using it. This can be a somewhat advanced tactic; save this for when you already feel comfortable using opinion openers on people around you.

Opinion Opener Example: Breast Enlargement

Opener: My friend's girlfriend is planning to have breast enlargement surgery as her birthday present to him. He doesn't know about this and I don't think he'll be happy. Should I say something to her? Or to him?

Typical Responses: Don't say anything / say something to her / say something to him [The content of her answer is irrelevant. Transition or continue with either or both follow-ons.]

Follow-on 1: Here's the thing, I think her real motivation might be that her sister just got her breasts done and they've always been really competitive. But would someone really change their body like that just out of jealousy?

Follow-on 2: I wonder if it's even my place to say something because I used to hook up with her sometimes – she's really beautiful but not my type, so I introduced her to my friend. I've tried to stay out of their relationship, but I don't want either of them to be unhappy.

Situational Openers

The Opener Risk/Reward Continuum					
Functional	Opinion	Situational	No Opener	Screening	Direct

A situational opener relates to something relevant to the environment in which you and a woman find yourselves. For example:

- What drink is that?

- Is that [celebrity name] over there?

- I love this music.

Most men who do not have access to the type of material you have in Magic Bullets use situational openers. Therefore, most attractive women have heard them literally hundreds, if not thousands, of times. Moreover, there are only a finite number of interesting conversational subjects that are likely to arise in standard places to meet women. Your odds of coming up with something that she has not heard before are pretty low.

For example, you may think that the situational opener, "where did you get that necklace/bracelet/ purse/ring/etc.?" could be original or interesting. However, most women will have heard this before and will think that it's far more likely that you are hitting on her than it is that you really care where she buys her jewelry. When was the last time you went up to a woman you didn't know and weren't attracted to and asked her about what she was wearing?

Guidelines for situational openers:

- If it isn't something that you would say to someone who you weren't attracted to, then don't say it to her. By definition, doing so would communicate interest.

- Hesitation is always bad when opening. It's especially damaging for situational openers, which rely on spontaneity. If you see a woman and plan to open situationally, do so right away.

- If you think of a situational opener once you have already chosen who to approach, then it likely won't come across as spontaneous. Save the opener for the next time the situation comes along.

- Like opinion openers, you can't walk across a room to open situationally; she will know that you did so to hit on her. If you're going to communicate your interest right away, you are better off using a direct opener (see below).

The primary advantage of a situational opener over an opinion opener is that your Transition (see Chapter 6) to other subjects will be easier. If a situational opener feels spontaneous and appropriate to her, you are much closer to a normal conversation than if you had opened her with a pretext, like with functional or opinion openers.

If you are generally good at improvisation, you can use these regularly. If not, use the other, more prepared, openers.

No Opener

The Opener Risk/Reward Continuum					
Functional	Opinion	Situational	No Opener	Screening	Direct

You actually don't have to use an opener. You can simply start talking to people. For example:

- You look just like my friend/little sister/cousin/niece/etc.

- Hi.

Or you can open in mid-conversation as if you already know them. Just start telling people a story as if they were your friends, without any explicit pretext for talking to them. Of course, this is risky because the group's natural reaction may be: "Why are you talking to us / telling us this?"

If you're going to try this type of "opener" – don't get tempted to try to communicate good qualities about yourself within the story (this is called embedding and is a valuable tool in other situations; see Chapter 18 on Storytelling). When a woman is actively wondering why you are talking to her, she will be more likely to interpret such a story as an amateurish and boastful attempt to hit on her.

I use a "no opener" opener if, and only if:

- I am in a high-energy environment.

- People are mingling freely.

- I am surrounded by other people and clearly being social.

The initial awkwardness and the difficulty of managing your credibility and keeping strangers' attention when they have no idea why you are talking to them make this a risky type of opener. At the same time, it's a high-reward opener if you pull it off because it displays a tremendous amount of confidence and social agility. If successfully executed, no transition will be necessary and you skip straight to the Attraction phase.

Screening Openers

The Opener Risk/Reward Continuum					
Functional	Opinion	Situational	No Opener	Screening	Direct

In a screening opener, you are making your intentions fairly clear. However, instead of forcing her to decide whether she is curious about you as in a direct opener, you imply that you are trying to decide whether you are interested in her. For example:

- Are you friendly?

- Is there more to you than meets the eye?

- I saw you from over there and wanted to see what you were like.

You can use these anytime, but they are best used in nighttime environments where flirting is on everybody's mind, such as bars and nightclubs. They work best with small groups, since many women will be reluctant to qualify themselves to you in front of their friends. Qualification is explained in Chapter 8; in this context, a woman qualifying herself to you means that she is telling you why you should be interested in her.

Despite the pretense that you are screening her, women know that most men would not approach them with this sort of challenge unless they were interested. So, screening openers are likely to communicate your intentions; however, if executed properly and in a playful tone, you will have a much better chance of winning her interest because you demonstrated confidence by approaching her in this way.

If you succeed with this kind of opener then you will find yourself in the Qualification phase. At this point it is safe to assume that attraction already exists. Later you will have to go back and fill in the blanks in her mind about who you are and why she is interested in you; however, it is easier to help someone who is already attracted to you figure out why she is attracted to you than it is to attract someone who is not already interested in you.

Direct Openers

The Opener Risk/Reward Continuum					
Functional	Opinion	Situational	No Opener	Screening	Direct

Direct openers are the highest-risk and offer the greatest reward. Such openers, popularized by Badboy Lifestyles (www.BadboyLifestyles.com), are especially useful when approaching a woman who is by herself. They are also popular in continental Europe and in other cultures where talking to strangers is not common. In such cultures, approaching a group of strangers will carry a high risk of failure whatever type of opener you use, so you may as well use a direct opener since it has the highest reward. The Badboy Lifestyles crew usually uses direct openers, even for women in groups.

These work, but only if your body language and tonality are very strong.

Examples of Direct Openers

- I like you. I want to get to know you.

- You're cute / attractive.

- You're the woman here I most want to meet.

Direct openers usually force a woman to decide whether she is interested in getting to know you.

However, she may know nothing about you except how you look, dress, and carry yourself, as well as the opener you just gave her. Thus, your initial verbal and your non-verbal communication must be very strong.

Your chances of quickly winning a woman's interest are better if you deliberately state your interest in her with a direct opener than if you clumsily betray your interest by delivering an opinion opener improperly. Most women will at least give you credit for your confidence if you "go direct." As we'll see in Chapter 7 (Attraction), confidence is one of the eight key "attraction switches" that make a woman interested. If you are successful, you move straight to a normal conversation without needing to Transition.

Still, I wouldn't recommend direct openers unless one of these three factors are present:

- Your skills are particularly advanced.

- You have taken a Badboy Lifestyles workshop (or something similar).

- You are approaching a woman who is by herself during the day and you could reasonably expect her to be attracted to you by your looks and non-verbal communication alone. If she's a supermodel and you're an average Joe, then you'll usually need time to make her interested in you based on your personality, and this time is best won with a more neutral opener such as an opinion opener.

Non-verbal elements in Approaching

It is a truism that non-verbal communication carries more weight than verbal communication. This is especially true in Approaching since a woman does not know much about you other than what you communicate by your non-verbal cues.

A key to success with all of these openers is to act as if you are simply a friendly, outgoing person, to whom talking to complete strangers is a normal everyday occurrence. If you set this sort of frame, people you talk to will be more likely to respond positively.

Before you Approach

Watch what you do before you Approach. Many women will notice you, consciously or subconsciously, before you start talking to them. Use this to your advantage. For example:

Before You Approach Checklist

✓ Be laughing, smiling, and having a good time.

✓ Display confident body language.

✓ Be the leader of whatever social group you are in (be making the biggest gestures, get the attention focused on you, etc.).

✓ Have women already around you. Having a couple of even average-looking women around you – even ones you met that night – will do wonders for your ability to interest a beautiful one. This is "pre-selection," another of the eight attraction triggers, explained in Chapter 7 (Attraction).

✓ Don't move around too much. The party is where you are.

✓ Don't look around too much. The party is where you are.

✓ Don't be obviously picking up women. Having them around and interested is great. Observably hitting on every woman in the bar is not.

✓ Being with cool people (even if you met them that night) also conveys high social value. Being the cool guy in a group of losers just makes you King of the Losers.

✓ Be social, not predatory. If you are staring around like a shark, looking for women to approach, they will notice and be defensive.

Watch for women already interested in you: Very little of what women do in social gatherings is random. When a group of women stops in a specific place, there's often a reason. And that reason is often a nearby man doing some of the things listed in the Before You Open Checklist. They want you to approach them. Similarly, a woman who makes repeated eye contact with you is likely inviting you to start a conversation with her. In this situation, use a higher risk/reward opener like No Opener, Screening, or Direct, since there is less need to try to fly "under the radar."

The First Few Seconds

When you see someone you are interested in, approach them right away. This has also been called the "3 second rule." Doing so will make your opener appear more spontaneous, she will not notice you hesitate, and you won't have time to make yourself more nervous. If you approach right away, you also don't have to worry about the group moving or becoming engaged in something else.

Women like confidence and spontaneity. They don't like to be stalked. Wandering around, circling her, looking at her, and trying to figure out what to say to her will just turn her off and creep her out. Get into the habit of seeing an attractive woman and approaching her group. You've already got a couple of openers ready, right?

Smile for the first few seconds. Don't grin like an eccentric goblin throughout the entire interaction, but smile as you approach the group and during the first few seconds of the opener. Smile with your eyes, not just your mouth.

Body Language and Tonality

Your opener should be loud enough that it cuts across whatever conversations the group is already having and gets their attention. Don't shout, but make it socially awkward for people not to pay attention to your opener. Practice speaking - loudly - from your chest, not your throat. If you put your hand on your chest, you should be able to talk in two ways: one in which you can feel the vibrations on your hand, and one where you can't. Train yourself to speak in the way where you can feel the vibrations. This will be a deeper, powerful, and more resonant voice.

Don't lean in. It makes you seem like you have lower status than the person you're talking to. Raise and project your voice enough that a woman can hear you from a normal standing position.

For opinion openers: Do not walk straight up to the group. Approach at an angle, tilt your head over your shoulders, and deliver your opener. Turn to face them within the first minute. Done correctly you can raise your value significantly by demonstrating that you do not need their attention or approval.

Approach Anxiety

Starting a conversation with a woman you don't know can be very scary. We call this fear "Approach Anxiety." Almost every man has it. We've learned how to deal with it and so will you.

If approach anxiety did not exist, bars and nightclubs would make a lot less money from liquor sales. Some men refer to alcohol as "liquid courage" and drink to lower their inhibitions and increase their confidence to approach women. Unfortunately, you cannot just send alcohol to the part of your brain that governs your inhibitions; it also goes to the parts of your brain that stop you from slurring, knocking things over, and remembering what just happened. Furthermore, if you depend on alcohol to get over approach anxiety, you will be restricting your opportunities for meeting women to those times and places where alcohol is easily accessible. Theoretically, you could walk around drunk all day meeting women. This might even be fun for a day or two. Actually it is fun. At my college, we called this "Spring Break." However, in normal life, if you're not going to constantly alter your brain chemistry with alcohol or other drugs, then you'll need to get over approach anxiety psychologically. This is hard, but necessary. Here are some ideas that may help:

Realize that rejection isn't bad

Approaching is a skill, not a personality test.

Before I learned to approach, I remember one night at a popular nightclub in San Diego when I approached 15 groups, and none of the conversations lasted for more than 2 minutes. I did not successfully approach a single group.

A few weeks later, I was out with someone who had learned from someone who knew what he was doing (he is currently an instructor with Love Systems). I saw how to approach effectively, and got a little bit better. With practice, I became proficient. Did I become a different person? No. I just learned to approach. No one was rejecting me during the awful 0 for 15 night. They were rejecting my approach, and rightly so since it was terrible. They could not possibly have been rejecting me, since no woman knew me for more than two minutes. They did not know anything about me. You as a person can no more be rejected by a woman after your opener than the game of basketball could reject you because you missed a shot. Practice the shot – or the opener – and you will succeed.

Go out somewhere where people don't know you and use a ridiculous opener – one that you expect would not work. Do it 10 times. You will not die. Instead, you should become less stressed and have more fun with the process. Keep that attitude when you use a "real" opener.

Get warmed up

Think of your first couple approaches as "warm ups." Most people generally need to ease into the process of being social with strangers. Before you go out, do things to get your social energy up. Call friends. Listen to high-energy music. Interact with random people. It's very difficult to go directly from being alone with your computer to being the life of the party.

Use opinion openers

Opinion openers are great for getting over approach anxiety because, after all, you're just asking a question. You're not hitting on anyone (yet). And because they are scripted, you can focus on their delivery. Good or bad delivery is usually what will make an opener work, so giving yourself a chance to focus on this – knowing that the content of your opener is fine – can only benefit you in the long run.

Create incentives

Very few people like approaching strangers. Some people set targets of a certain number of approaches per day or per week. Others take it a step further and create systems to reward themselves if they succeed or punish themselves if they fail. For example, the Venusian Arts Handbook suggests that you go out with a friend and give him $200 and have him give you $20 back every time you open someone new. Or you can tell your friend not to drive you home until you've opened 8 new groups.

Dealing with other men

Don't be afraid of mixed groups (groups with men and women in them). Mixed groups are actually easier than all-female groups if you are using an opinion opener, since you can (and usually should) direct your opening conversation at the men in a group. If you are sufficiently interesting, the women will want to also get your attention. By playfully ignoring or teasing the woman you're interested in, you may start to create the type of emotional tension that often leads to attraction. See Chapter 7.

You can and should approach mixed groups even when such groups include more men than women. The relationships between the men and women in such groups will become obvious early in your interaction with them (or will become so when you ask how everyone knows each other), and you will earn credit with the women in the group for having the guts to approach when most other men would be too timid.

Do not initiate conflict with the other men in the group. A woman will be less interested in you if she senses that you cannot get along with the men in her life. If you appear to disrespect a woman's brother, sister's boyfriend, coworker, platonic male friend, or any other man in her social circle, you will demonstrate poor social skills. You will also end up making enemies within her social circle, who will try to convince her not to date you.

Befriending other men does not mean kissing up to them – neither they, nor the women in the group, will be interested in you if you do – but it does mean treating them with respect. Imagine that you are at the park with your younger sister. What would a man have to do for you to want her to date him, or at least for you to be neutral about it? One technique for bonding with someone is to act as if he is already your friend. Act toward other men in her group as you would act around your own friends.

Sports, gadgets (comparing cell phones often works), cars, alcohol, and movies are often good sources of conversation with other men.

Now, that being said, how does approaching a mixed group differ from approaching an all-female group?

- Address the men in the group primarily, at least at first.

- Quickly find out how they all know each other (so you know which women in the group are single and which have their boyfriends or husbands in the group).

- Use an opener that is more about events and actions and less about emotions and "getting a woman's opinion."

If the other men in the group have just met the women that night, then they are your potential rivals. If they are competing with you for the woman you want, ignore them. If they are hitting on her friends and doing so competently, then befriend them. They are now your "wingmen" and you will likely sink or swim together. See Chapter 21 on Winging for advanced strategies on how to work with other men so you all succeed.

Chapter 6: Transitioning

6

IN THIS CHAPTER

- Transitions within the model

- Content Transitions

- Observational Transitions

- Phrasal Transitions

- No Transition

Transitions within the model

Transitions bridge the gap between the Approaching phase and Attraction phase. To begin Attraction, your conversation with a woman and/or her group must have reached the point where you have the freedom to discuss a variety of subjects and to express emotion. We call this sort of interaction a normal conversation. Once you are able to begin a normal conversation, the Transitioning phase is complete.

Sometimes you will have this freedom immediately after Approaching. For example, if you use a direct opener such as "I like you. I want to get to know you," and she responds positively, you are in position to have a normal conversation. The next subject you talk about could be virtually anything, and you don't need a transition.

If, however, you have asked her for the time (a functional opener; the lowest on the risk-reward scale), you don't necessarily have the freedom to move straight from that to talking about personal subjects. Generally, the lower risk-reward profile of the opener you use, the more work you will have to do in the Transition.

Let's look at the four general types of transitions available to you.

Content Transitions

A content transition uses the response to your opener to change the subject to a new conversation. For example, if you were using the "my friend Eddie who just broke up with his girlfriend and wants to date her friend" opener from Chapter 5, she might mention that her best friend back home in London had recently been in a similar situation.

If you're quick, you might see an immediate content transition opportunity here, and interrupt her by confirming that she's from London. When she tells you that she is, you can roll out a London-related anecdote. It doesn't even have to be long, but it has to be interesting enough that she pursues that conversation instead of the one about Eddie. Going back to talking about Eddie is going back a phase, not forward.

This dialogue may help explain:

> **Me:** *My friend Eddie over there in the green shirt just broke up with his girlfriend. How long do you think he has to wait before asking her friend out?*
>
> **Her:** *Umm, I don't know. My best friend Jane back home in London was in that situation with two guys. She'd been dating one...*
>
> **Me:** *[interrupting] You're from London? Oh my God, I just got back from there. I had the greatest time.*
>
> **Her:** *What were you doing in London?*

...and away we go into Attraction (Chapter 7).

Was that too easy? Alright, let's pretend that she didn't ask what I was doing in London, but returns back to the subject of Eddie. This might mean that she is responding to my opinion opener out of a sense of social obligation and isn't especially interested in me yet. Or it might mean that she is more interested in Eddie's situation than in my impressions of London. Or it might not mean anything at all. It doesn't matter. Have the stronger frame and ensure that the conversation moves forward, not backward. Let's pick the conversation up from where I interrupted her.

> **Me:** *[interrupting] You're from London? Oh my God, I just got back from there. I had the greatest time.*
>
> **Her:** *Yeah, so Jane ended up deciding that she couldn't even be friends with either of them and...*
>
> **Me:** *[interrupting]: Isn't it crazy the way people with British accents sound more educated?*
>
> *My friend just opened a restaurant in Mayfair and even the foreign cleaning staff sound like Harvard PhDs, even when they were talking about mops and tables. Did you ever notice that?*
>
> **Her:** *Yeah, kind of, but I haven't been there in ages.*
>
> **Me:** *Oh yeah? Well, I loved London. We went on this helicopter ride over the city, and...*

...and away we go into Attraction (Chapter 7).

By the way, you don't have to interrupt to make a content transition work. But you shouldn't reach back into the conversation to find your content transition. For example, assume that we continued talking about Jane and Eddie for a while. A few minutes later, it would not feel as natural to start talking about London. It might look like I was grasping at ways to keep the conversation going, which could telegraph my interest in her before I've had much of a chance to attract her. Again, as we covered in Chapter 5, it's not necessarily bad for a woman to see right away that you are interested in her. It's only bad if you're pretending not to be, using an opinion opener.

A more advanced tactic is to create the conditions for a content transition within the opener. For example, after you ask about Eddie's situation, and she gives her initial response, you can mention that you and Eddie were just talking about this on the airplane earlier that day and he told you that... [insert more details from the situation]. We call the reference to the airplane an "open thread" and cover this concept in detail in Chapter 18 on Storytelling. If she asks about the airplane or where you were traveling from, then she has opened the door for a content transition.

To be good at content transitions, you need good improvisational and conversational skills, and should convey enough enthusiasm about the new topic to carry the conversation and your listener(s) with you.

Observational Transitions

An observational transition can occur when you notice, apparently spontaneously, something about a woman or her group. This observation should still be more or less neutral, although it may give you an opportunity to tease her about it later.

For an observational transition to work, you must sell your listener(s) on the idea that you really noticed something about them and that this wasn't planned all along. Delivery is key here.

Observational transitions are often connected to cold reads. Cold reading is the art of telling people truisms about human nature in a way that seems like it is tailored to them. Here are a couple of examples:

To a single woman:

I bet you that when most people meet you, they think you're harsh. But I don't think that's the truth. My intuition is that you are actually shy, so when you meet new people, you put up walls.

To two women:

Alright, it seems that you [pick one of them at random] are the good one and you [point at the other woman] are the bad one. And that's okay. One of you can be my angel and the other can be the devil. Like we'll roll down the street, one of you on each arm, we'll make all the other women jealous, and every time there's a decision to be made, you guys can whisper in my ear and we'll see who's more tempting.

Phrasal Transition

A phrasal transition is really "No Transition" with crutches. The crutch is that you say something to connect the Approaching phase and the Attraction phase like:

- That reminds me of...

- That's just like when...

- Yeah, that's crazy, because...

You can use these even if there is no connection between the subject of your opener and what you're about to say next (which will be in the Attraction phase). Usually there won't be.

No Transition

Using No Transition means simply starting to talk about an unrelated topic. This may feel strange or awkward. In truth, most people -- especially women -- don't care if there is little obvious relationship between different conversational topics, as long as they are entertained. Think about a stand-up comedian. His jokes will be grouped into certain subjects, but these subjects are rarely related. So after a couple of jokes about, say, airlines, he or she will tell a couple about some movie star. They're not connected, but we don't notice or care. We're entertained and interested.

That being said, it does sometimes feel awkward to her, and the fact that it may feel awkward to you will affect your non-verbal communication or the reaction of others in her group. Even if you can get away without a transition, why bother? You don't get any points for skipping the phase and it only takes a few seconds anyway.

Observation Transition Example: The Best Friends Test

If I have approached a group of two women, then I will often use the Best Friends Test. Credit "Style."

My version has evolved from his – not necessarily better or worse – and with repeated use, your version of any routine should evolve into one that feels comfortable and natural to you. So focus on the underlying direction of this routine as opposed to memorizing it word-for-word. Text in square brackets [like this] refers to explanations of what is going on or what I might be thinking.

Me: [interrupting at some point during the opener] You guys have known each other for a while, haven't you?

Them: [whatever answer they give is irrelevant, unless I want to use it for a Content Transition.]

Me: I noticed that you have [slight pause] the exact same smile.

Them: Laughter [If they're not laughing, your delivery was probably off.]

Me: Here, I'm going to show you something cool...

do you guys [pause] use the same shampoo? / have the same favorite color? / [anything that relates to a commonality].

[We need to explore some contingencies here, as women will usually do one of three different things at this point: They will both look at each other. Or one will look at the other. Or both will keep looking straight ahead at me.]
If they look at each other...

Me: [Wave hand between them at their eye level toget their attention]. You guys looked at each other before even answering the question. [Pause – they will turn to look at each other again.] You just did it again. [They laugh and look at each other again.]

And again. [They will look at each other yet again and laugh. You can do this several times if you really want to, but once or twice is enough.] You see, people who share a strong emotional connection will turn to look at each other when asked a question about shared experiences, even over something as mundane as shampoo [or colors].

If only one looks at the other:

Me: See, she's the dominant one in this friendship because you [indicating the one who looked at the other] looked at her first. [They will almost certainly laugh or talk here. Let them for a second and then turn to the 'dominant' one.] So if she's getting out of line, I'll bring her to you. [By the way, this isn't an especially accurate predictor of social dominance between two women. I invented this a couple of years ago and in that time it's been accurate about two- thirds of the time. Treat this as fun, not as a meaningful psychological test.]

If they both look at you:

Me: Interesting. Normally people who share an emotional connection will turn to look at each other when asked a question about shared experiences. Either you're both really unique and independent people or you don't actually like each other very much. [Usually by then they look at each other, and then I'll catch them on it, and tease them with something like:]
"I knew you had it in you" or "I knew you guys liked each other deep down."

Advanced notes for the Best Friends Test:

You can get away with telling either or both women that they are looking at each other even if they are not. Or if they only make a quick glance out of the corner of their eye and don't even move their head. I've even gotten away with telling them that they were looking at each other when neither woman's eyes moved, but this doesn't always work. That's why I created the contingencies for when one or both of them doesn't turn to look at her friend.

Right after "Here, I'm going to show you something really cool" is an excellent opportunity to drop in a false time constraint (Chapter 5) like "and then I should get back to my friends." It is also a good opportunity to rearrange your physical dynamics. Usually at this point, when I've told them I'm going to show them "something cool" I move them so they are beside each other, facing me, and I am comfortably standing or leaning against a wall, bar, countertop, etc. We call this "locking in" and discuss it further in Chapter 18.

7

IN THIS CHAPTER

Attraction within the model

The Attraction phase is where you – guess what? – get the woman you are interested in attracted to you. The Attraction phase begins as soon as you are able to have a normal conversation (see Glossary) with a woman and her group. This occurs immediately if you meet a woman through your social circle (Chapter 12). If she is a stranger, it occurs after Transitioning or after an opener that does not require a transition (Chapters 5 and 6).

The phase ends when she becomes interested or curious about you as a man and a potential romantic and/or sexual interest. Repeat that: "As a man." Not as a friend. Not as a clownish guy that has been weirdly entertaining. As a man.

To explain how this works, we use a concept called Value. No, this is not your intrinsic value as a person. Your value is just how desirable you are at a specific moment to a specific woman. A woman's value is based on how desirable she feels to men in general. When your value is greater than hers, she will usually become attracted to you.

You will know that you have reached this point because she will let you qualify her (see Chapter 8). You can measure your progress to this goal by looking out for specific Signs of Attraction, discussed in the final section of this chapter.

The best way to create attraction is for her to discover things about your personality that she likes.

This increases your value. We refer to the process as Demonstrating or a Demonstration of Higher Value and use the acronym DHV both as a noun and as a verb. Because Attraction is an early phase and you probably haven't learned much about her personality and likes and dislikes, you should usually look for opportunities to DHV on the universally attractive characteristics from Chapter 3.

The Attraction phase should take approximately 2-20 minutes and you will be doing most of the talking. Try to get through it as quickly as possible. The reason we call it the Emotional Progression Model is that you are meant to guide a woman through a progression of different emotions until you reach your goal. Serving up an endless stream of Attraction material will not get you there, unless she is drunk, desperate, or consciously seeking a one-night stand.

Another reason to move quickly is that interactions with strangers can end suddenly and without warning. Her friends might show up or make her leave, she could get an important phone call, or something else might require her attention. As you'll see in Chapters 9 and 22, to be reasonably sure of seeing a woman again, you should make sure that you at least get to the Comfort phase in your first interaction with her. Since you don't know how much time you'll have to do this, don't waste any.

Final Note: Attraction for a man is like an on/off switch. Most men are either attracted to someone or they are not. For a woman, attraction is a continuous process, like putting air in a balloon. Doing things that create attraction is like blowing air in the balloon. When you "tone it down" and stop blowing into the balloon it will gradually and imperceptibly leak air. If you let enough air leak out without refilling it, the attraction becomes stale. It's extremely hard to rebuild it at this stage; she'll go looking for other balloons instead. Make sure you periodically refresh her attraction to you throughout your interaction with her, even after the Attraction phase.

A woman's value

As we saw above, a woman's value is based on her desirability to men in general. It has nothing to do with how desirable you think she is. Most men, shallow beasts that we are, respond primarily to a woman's physical attractiveness, making her value closely tied to her looks. Actually, her value will be based on her perception of her looks, which is affected by such factors as her self-esteem, her previous experiences with men, and how she feels she compares with other women.

In fact, the more attractive a woman, the greater the influence of unpredictable factors such as her self-esteem. Some extremely beautiful women have an amazing psychological challenge to keep their heads on straight. From an early age, they learn that many rules don't apply to them. Men will give them access to high-status social events, money, and excitement that most women their age never get. This can raise a woman's self-esteem if she takes these things seriously, or lower it if she doesn't feel she deserves them. Beautiful women can find themselves irrationally hated by other women, and other people often treat them as if they are one-dimensional sex objects. Unless they have strong personalities or strong family and peer networks, many extremely attractive women end up a little bit loopy. Some pretty women think they are bombshells. Some bombshells think they are average. Some actually think they are ugly and focus on their perceived flaws.

Moreover, a woman's value can change quite rapidly based on her social context. Put an attractive woman in a room full of plain women and she may feel beautiful. Put her in a room full of supermodels and she may feel average. She may feel beautiful again if she gets a job waitressing at a trendy club and routinely flirts with high-value men – until she gets off work. A new outfit or a haircut may raise her value. Seeing her ex-boyfriend with a beautiful woman may lower it. And so on. One of the reasons why beautiful women are often insecure is that their friends are often beautiful as well. A woman may not feel beautiful in comparison.

All of this serves to illustrate that a woman's value might be very different from how attractive you think she is.

A man's value

When you first meet a woman, she will assume that you have roughly the same value as other men she has met in similar situations. If you are a stranger approaching her at a bar, she may notice your clothes, body language, and general appearance, but she is likely to lump you in with the armies of low-value strangers who have approached her at bars before. She will assume you have low value until you prove her wrong. This partly explains why many women will be more curious about a man in an exclusive VIP section of a difficult-to-get-into lounge than about someone at a generic bar. You probably think this way too. Imagine meeting someone at Steven Spielberg's house. All things being equal, you would probably assume that they have more going for them than someone you met on a street corner.

Nonetheless, the social context in which you meet a woman is not an insurmountable obstacle. This chapter gives you the tools to change a woman's impression of you very quickly. And even if you do meet someone at Steven Spielberg's house, you will often still need to increase your value. Like many other species, males traditionally parade in front of females, and females choose who they want. As the "chooser," a woman will generally feel that her value is higher than most men's.

Disqualification

We saw above that raising your value involves communicating your attractive qualities to a woman.

If she feels that you are bragging, she may become turned off as well as skeptical of what you are saying. Women are more likely to pay attention to your good qualities if they feel that they are figuring them out for themselves.

One important technique is to DHV in a subtle and indirect way. We cover this in the second half of this chapter, starting with "How to DHV." Still, such techniques can be less likely to work if a woman thinks that you are hitting on her. You need to clear the ground first.

One way we do this is through a technique we call disqualification. Disqualification means that we say or do something that someone who was interested in her would not likely say or do. This convinces her that we are not hitting on her, and this, amusingly, is what actually allows us to hit on her effectively. She'll thank you for this later.

There are three elements of a good disqualifier. First, it should be a choice. You are choosing not to be interested in her. Second, it should be positive. You're not disqualifying her because of anything bad about her (unless it's obviously teasing, as in the fourth example below). It should never be an insult. Third, it should be surmountable. You will want her to be able to win you over later. Telling her that you are married with three children is neither a choice nor is it a surmountable obstacle. Here are some better disqualifiers:

- "You're fun; too bad you're not my type."

- "My girlfriend" (In the context of any story that takes place in the past - surmount this later by saying that she was your girlfriend at the time the story took place).

- "I love women who are tall/short/blonde/Asian/preppy" (something she is not).

- "You and I would not get along" (said while smiling).

Disqualification also conveys value in itself. It helps you appear Challenging. An effective disqualifier should also:

- Be understood by her entire group, so that they do not try to "protect" her from you.

- Occur early in the Attraction phase. The longer you talk to an attractive woman without disqualifying yourself, the more people will think you are hitting on her.

Disqualification does not always come through statements. Sometimes you can accomplish the same goals non-verbally, by employing neutral or dismissive body language in situations where an interested man's physical posture would betray his intentions. Or sometimes you can disqualify yourself by simply not doing something, such as not looking over and smiling if she touches you, not focusing on her to the exclusion of the group, or not buying her a drink when she requests it.

Disqualification theory can easily take a whole book in itself. More advanced game can involve disqualifying during the Opener, or the use of "negs."

Negs

Negs have a very limited and specific use and purpose. We present them as a potential tool, but you can enjoy great success with women without them.

A neg is a very strong disqualification tool that can also raise your value. A neg is something that appears to be communicated with positive or at least neutral intent toward a woman, but "inadvertently" betrays that you notice that she is not perfect. For example, the classic neg, "nice nails, are they real?" is somewhat of a compliment, until she admits that her nails are fake. "You blink a lot" (said neutrally) or "your nose wiggles when you talk" (said as if you think it's cute) accomplish the same thing.

An effective neg will:

- Disqualify yourself. Men who are hitting on a woman don't generally do this kind of thing. She'll know it and her friends will know it.

- Temporarily lower her value, decreasing the potential value gap between you.

- Increase your value. Low-value men don't often say those sorts of things to high-value women. Low-value men do insult unattainable women, but these are negs, not insults.

The problem with negs is that they can often backfire if used inappropriately and demonstrate low Social Intuition. Here are some tips to avoid this situation:

Only neg high-value women. If she is not one of the most attractive women in the room, don't neg her.

Don't over-neg. One, maybe two, is usually the maximum unless you are dealing with a woman who is vastly out of your league.

Don't draw attention to the neg. Change the subject quickly or deliver the neg as an aside when you are in the middle of a longer story or piece. You should always say something unrelated to the neg as soon as you deliver it. If you pause for her to react, she might feel defensive or feel she needs to respond negatively to you in order to "save face," especially in front of her friends. Psychologically, she will often actually adopt that negative attitude to you, and your chances with her will diminish.

How to DHV

There are five basic ways to DHV. I have ranked these below, in order from most to least effective, with a hypothetical example for each based on the characteristic "Status":

1.
- **She observes it.**
  She sees me come to an exclusive new restaurant in a limousine and the Maitre D' ushers me to the best table.

2.
- **She learns of it from a trusted personal source, like a friend.**
  Her best friend tells her that I am friends with the owner of the restaurant.

3.
- **She learns of it from a neutral source.**
  She sees a picture of me with the owner of the restaurant.

4.
- **She learns of it from a source that is biased to me, like my friend.**
  My friend tells her that I am friends with the owner of the restaurant.

5.
- **I tell her.**
  I tell her that I am friends with the owner of the restaurant.

Let's explore each of these in more detail before applying them to our eight universally positive characteristics from Chapter 3.

Observed DHVs

In most cases, it is preferable that a woman observe your DHVs as opposed to learning about them from someone else or being told about them. We always value what our own eyes and ears tell us. Unfortunately, this is not always possible. For example, it can be difficult to have a woman Observe Pre-selection (see Chapter 3) when there are no other women around.

What we used to call Interactive Value Demonstrations – demonstrating value by doing something like making a woman laugh or teaching her something – are Observed DHVs.

Learned DHVs

If you can't have a woman Observe something, the next best thing is for her to Learn it from another source. The closer this source is to her, the more weight the DHV will have. We'll look at the three primary types of sources below, from the highest-impact (and hardest to execute) to lowest-impact (but easiest):

> *Personal source:* Personal source DHVs can come spontaneously if a woman's friends like you, so it's important to befriend and impress her group. You can also try to help this process along by DHVing to her friends and hoping they tell her. However, you will want to avoid attracting or appearing to be hitting on her friends, as this may cause the woman you are interested in to become unresponsive to you. This can be solved with a good wingman (see Chapter 21) who can tell her friends good things about you. Personal source DHVs are also much easier to obtain within your social circle (Chapter 12).

> *Neutral source:* Neutral sources are those which a woman presumes not to be aligned with either you or her, e.g., random strangers, coffee shop owners, internet websites, etc. You can make these work for you if you plan ahead. For example, a friendly coffee shop owner who sees you regularly might be persuaded to relay some helpful anecdotes about you when you're in the bathroom. When you meet a woman at a social venue who is attached, make a good impression anyway. She may see you later on talking to another woman and tell her how wonderful you are. Or she might have desirable single friends and give you Personal source DHVs when talking to them about you.

> *Biased source:* Most women will put more weight into what your friends say about you than in what you say about yourself. This is true even though she presumes your friends to be "on your side." Biased source DHVs are also very useful in conveying attractive attributes like wealth. If you tell a woman that you are rich, it's likely to turn her off. If your friend tells her, she's more likely to take note. In general, if I'm at a party with a friend and meet someone interesting, I might introduce her to my friend

and then drift off for a while. The next time I see her, my friend will likely have raised my value to her by talking about me.

Told DHVs

The Told DHV is the workhorse of Attraction. It's the most versatile of the communication types, and is often your only option if the situation is not right for an Observed or Learned DHV. By far the biggest challenge in doing this is avoiding any appearance of bragging. Bragging implies insecurity, which implies a lack of Confidence and Social Intuition.

Storytelling, especially the technique known as embedding, is your most useful tool here. We cover this subject in greater detail in Chapter 17; however, since it is crucial for Told DHVs, we've included a short section here.

An embedded DHV is a DHV that appears to be relevant to the overall story without appearing to be the primary purpose of the story. See how many embedded DHVs you can find in the fictional story below:

> My ex-girlfriend picked me up at the airport this morning. Normally she drives an Audi, but today she shows up in a red Maserati. She didn't say anything about it, so I pretended that I didn't notice, just to irritate her.
>
> But then about 5 minutes outside the airport, we got pulled over by the police. The license plate wasn't valid, the registration on the car wasn't hers, and neither was the insurance. I whispered to her "Karen, you'd tell me if you all of a sudden became a drug lord, right?"
>
> That's when she finally explained that they'd given her the car to use for this photo shoot she was doing, and even though she's not supposed to be driving it off the set, she thought it would be fun to pick me up in it. It took 2 hours to sort it out with the police.
>
> I feel badly because she's going to be in a lot of trouble, but the moral of the story is that even though it's fun to drive a Maserati, it's not that fun to be on the side of the road for two hours surrounded by like eight police cars. You look pretty sketchy. People were stopping to take pictures.

Don't use this story. For one thing, it didn't happen to you. For another, it's designed to show how to embed DHVs, not how to construct a great Attraction story. How many of these embedded DHVs did you notice?

- The narrator has an ex-girlfriend. He's not a total loser.

- He is close enough to his ex-girlfriend that she would pick him up at the airport.

- He has a lifestyle which allows him to travel (he's coming from the airport).

- His ex-girlfriend has an Audi. This doesn't necessarily give her a ton of value, but it gives her a little bit, which gives him some value by implication.

- His ex-girlfriend does photo shoots. She must be attractive.

- His ex-girlfriend does the kind of photo shoots in which she'd have a Maserati for the day on the set. She must be very attractive.

There are two key rules to follow when embedding DHVs. First, the story must still be interesting, even if you took out all the embedded DHVs. Second, each embedded DHV should be very relevant to the story. Err on the side of caution; it's better to undersell your embedded DHVs than it is to be seen as bragging.

DHVs by characteristic

Armed with these tools, we can now proceed through each of the eight characteristics from Chapter 3 and look for appropriate and effective ways to communicate them. Some general patterns:

- The foundational characteristics (Health, Social Intuition, Humor) are nearly always Observed, and difficult to communicate any other way.

- The attribute characteristics (Power and Status, Wealth) are more flexible. If they can be Observed in a socially-acceptable way, they can be very powerful. Otherwise, they are often Learned.

- The outcome characteristics (Confidence, Pre-selected, Challenging) are primarily Observable, although Pre-selection lends itself to being Told or Learned (Biased source).

DHV Impact by Communication Path

	DHVs	Observed	Learned: personal source	Learned: neutral source	Learned: biased source	Told
Foundational Characteristics	Health	High	Medium-low	Medium-low	Medium-low	Medium-low
	Social Intuition	High	Low	Low	Low	Low
	Humor	High	Low	Low	Low	Low
Attributes	Status	High	High	High	High	High
	Wealth	Medium	High	High	High	Medium
Outcomes	Confident	High	Low	Low	Low	No
	Pre-selected	High	Medium	Med-low	High	High
	Challenging	High	Low	Low	Med-low	Low

Health

Health is generally Observed. If you have a nice body, show it off in a way that's fashionable. Health can be Learned or Told, but this will only have an impact if it reinforces her perception from looking at you. Embedding a phrase about mountain climbing or leading a whitewater rafting trip into a larger story may get her attention, but if she cannot observe signs of your good health, then it will not likely resonate with her.

Social Intuition

Social Intuition is also almost always Observed. As soon as you meet a woman, she will subconsciously evaluate your social skills. If she notices you before you interact with her, she will observe your Social Intuition in the context of your interactions with other people. So make sure your social presence is always "on." If you're at a social venue like a party or a nightclub, always be with people and having a good time. Don't circle around looking for women to meet.

The very act of being able to enter a group of strangers and lead a conversation for several minutes demonstrates Social Intuition.

Your energy level is also a manifestation of Social Intuition. Have an air of excitement, an energy level slightly greater than hers, and a genuine passion for meeting people. Enthusiasm is contagious. Notice the effect on your game when you go out with confident, high-energy people.

Humor

Humor is almost always Observed. If you find it difficult to be humorous in the first few minutes of meeting someone, try role-play or other silly games. For example, you can tell a woman in mid-conversation that you are breaking up with her and getting a divorce if you disagree with something she says. Make this playful. Then when she says something you like, ask her to marry you again. Then divorce her later and argue about who gets the DVD collection. Or, if she tells you that she likes skiing, start planning your trip to North Pole Mountain together. While you're there, you can steal Santa's list so that he'll give both of you Switzerland for Christmas so you'll both be able to ski whenever you want. It's immature, but it's fun. And most women will take "immature and fun" over "mature and serious" when they first meet a man[4]. There are literally hundreds of examples of these - written word-for-word the way I and other Love Systems Instructors use them, in the Love Systems Routines Manual (www.LoveSystems.com/Routines).

Status

With Status, we enter into the Attributes. You have more flexibility in communicating these than you do with the Foundational characteristics.

Having a woman observe Status can best be done either through a demonstration of genuine Status that you possess (for example, breezing through the line at a hot nightclub) or through the assistance of your friends. When you are trying to attract a woman, your friends should be as deferential to you as possible, unless they are trying to date her friends, in which case overly submissive behavior will hurt them. Your friends can randomly appear over the course of the interaction thanking you, in front of her, for getting them into some party, for giving them a job, or for anything else that would imply that you have Status.

If you are using Told DHVs to convey Status, the following elements can serve as useful ideas for embedding:

- Friends/associates who jump at a moment's notice to do something with or for you because of their respect for you or ties to you.

---

[4] *Advanced readers may notice the "push-pull" dynamic here, which also builds attraction. And of course there is no such thing as North Pole Mountain. That's what makes it fun.*

- Your career (if applicable).

- People you know (be careful to avoid "name dropping").

Wealth

Demonstrating Wealth by having a woman Observe it can be tricky. Going out of your way to show off can come across as crude, showing low Social Intuition and possibly implying that you are compensating for deficiencies elsewhere in your life. For example, in some cultures, certain very expensive sports cars, especially small ones, can carry this implication.

When a woman observes a man's Wealth, she will take everything in: how he dresses, what kind of car he drives, where he lives, etc. If you are not well-off, make the most of what you have. Put a large bill, like a $100 bill in the United States, around a stack of smaller bills to create a roll that appears to represent Wealth. Keep what you do own in good repair. And remember – Wealth includes future prospects. A medical student probably doesn't have much Wealth right now, but will be considered to have a high Wealth value by most women.

One of the worst ways to demonstrate Wealth is to go out of your way to spend it on her. Don't make a show of buying her drinks or taking her somewhere very expensive on the first date. If a woman feels that you are trying to attract her with money, she may wonder whether this is because you have nothing else going for you. If you spend a lot on her, she might deliberately withhold sex, in hope of more money being spent on her in the future or in order not to feel like a prostitute. See Chapter 16 for more details about money and dating.

In contrast, if a woman asks you to buy her a drink when you first meet her, she's not testing for Wealth. She's either not interested in you at all and is just looking for free drinks and the opportunity to feel desirable, or she's testing to see if you are Challenging (see below).

Told DHVs on Wealth can be difficult to pull off; the embedding must be very subtle. Learned DHVs are usually much better. Other people have complete freedom to comment on your Wealth even though you don't.

Confident

Confidence, like Health, is best Observed. Women aren't consciously and intellectually looking for Confident men, as many are for men who have Status or Wealth.

Women look for the emotional impact that a Confident man has on her. This usually requires her to experience your Confidence first-hand. Confidence can be communicated by:

- Approaching without hesitation.

- Making strong eye contact.

- Speaking with a slow, measured pace .

- Speaking loudly.

- Standing up straight with your shoulders back and relaxed.

- Standing with your feet at least shoulder-width apart.

- Keeping your hands accessible and relaxed. Avoid too many gestures or hiding your hands in your pockets or behind your back.

- Avoiding defensive maneuvers (e.g. holding a drink in front of your chest).

- Moving in a relaxed, slow manner.

As you can see from the above list, Confidence is often conveyed non-verbally. Non-verbal communication is covered in greater detail in Chapter 18.

Nothing on the list is particularly original. But at any given bar or party, I see more than half of the men there displaying major body language problems that prevent them from succeeding with women. Every Love Systems live training workshop we run has the same issue at first. If you are not perceived as Confident, you will have zero chance with many women. Of course, being Confident does not mean being arrogant or never admitting failure or vulnerabilities.

Do you remember the shy kid who gets the girl in teen movies? Sixteen Candles is a classic example.

The real world is different – the main character in that movie would never get a girlfriend at his high school. Every time you see a TV show or movie in which a male character asks a woman "so… um… would you like to… you know… go out with me on Saturday?" and she says yes, remind yourself that this is fiction. In real life, being shy and nervous – no matter how cute or how much the tortured artist you think you are being – is a terrible way to make a woman attracted to you.

Pre-selected

In large social gatherings, such as parties or nightclubs, take advantage of the opportunity to meet lots of women. Some of them will come back to you later, including when you are talking to other women. I may be talking to two women and realize that neither is right for me romantically. At some point, the three of us can approach another group. The fact that I already have women with me gives some value through Pre-selection (even if we're obviously not involved) and carries a nice side bonus of getting on the good side of whatever men happen to be in the second group. Or you can just bring attractive female friends out with you who will help you meet other women.

Keep in mind that Pre-selection is also affected by a woman's assessment of other women's value. Hanging around with a drunk and unattractive woman who has been kissing every man in the nightclub does not make you Pre-selected.

Pre-selection can also work as a Learned DHV (usually from a Biased source) or a Told DHV. A couple of stories about your ex-girlfriends are often a good way of doing this. Don't go overboard. It's not normal for a man to talk at great length about his ex-girlfriends to people he just met. They may think that you have low Social Intuition or that you're obsessed with your past and not ready for a new relationship.

Challenging

Being a Challenge is crucially important. In fact, one of the main purposes of the Qualification phase (which is coming next) is to confirm to her that you are Challenging. This DHV is usually Observed, similar to and for the same reasons as with Confidence.

If you're not a Challenge, most women will be skeptical about your other qualities. It doesn't fit that a man who, for example, has Status and Social Intuition would be easily won over. Especially before a woman has done much to convey her attractive qualities (this happens in Qualification).

Another reason to be Challenging is that it makes the process more fun for a woman. An attractive woman can have men, even very attractive men, all the time. This is boring. When other men fawn over her but you don't, it's more interesting for her to try to get your attention and "convert" you than it is to play a game that's already won.

Even if she doesn't know enough about you to be attracted yet, being a Challenge can intrigue her. Why aren't you hitting on her? Are you gay or taken? Or are you a high-value man who has plenty of high-quality options? Now she's curious.

As noted above, sometimes women will test to see if you are Challenging. One common way to do this is to ask you to buy them a drink. Don't. It's not about the money; she knows that almost any man can afford a drink. She is more likely testing you to see if you will stand up to her. If you don't, she may think you are weak or have nothing going for you other than money. However, if you are ordering a drink anyway while you are talking to her, offer her one. It's polite, and it's a social convention; you will lose Social Intuition points if you don't.

Signs of Attraction

While the ultimate test of whether she is attracted to you is whether she will let you Qualify her, there are some intermediate signs we can be looking for. Different women do different things when they are attracted to a man, but the below list shows some of the more common signs of attraction:

- She reinitiates conversation when you stop talking.

- She giggles.

- She touches you.

- She plays with / tosses her hair.

- She asks you for your name or any other personal questions (e.g., age, where you live).

- She disagrees with you but laughs when she does.

- She compliments you on anything.

- She asks if you have a girlfriend or mentions your girlfriend, whether or not you've said you have one.

- She calls you a player or a heartbreaker.

- She introduces you to her friends.

- She is laughing, smiling, and/or holding eye contact with you.

- Passive signs (see below).

Passive signs

Passive signs are indicators of a different type. Instead of doing something to convey attraction, she shows her interest in you by not doing something that she would otherwise do if she weren't attracted. For example, she might stay to talk to you when her friends go to the bathroom. Even the very act of spending a significant amount of time with you (generally over 30 minutes) at a busy, exciting nightclub could be a passive sign.

Caveats

No sign is definitive. A woman can do some of the things on this list without being attracted to you, or she can engage in none of them and still be attracted. These are guides, not laws of physics.

It is easy to get addicted to signs of attraction. They feel good, and if you're not used to them, they feel like little wins ("This beautiful woman is actually attracted to me!"). However, inducing too many of these signs without moving on to Qualification is counterproductive, and gets boring for women. The end goal of a sexual relationship is more exciting than these signs anyway.

Iealousy

Jealousy is simply Pre-selection brought from an abstract to a specific level. In the abstract, a woman may know that other women are interested in you, and this may make her curious about you. At the specific level, she sees other women demonstrating interest in you right now. Why is this a good thing?

- It helps keep the interaction fresh and exciting and challenging.

- It is an antidote against her perceiving you as a potential "orbiter" (See Chapter 9).

- It is a strong emotion. Women like experiencing ranges of emotions. Feeling jealousy and then feeling reassured has much more of an effect on a woman than just feeling happy.

- It warns her that she can't play "hard to get" forever. Other women are staking their claim, so she'd better move on you before it's too late. This makes your job in the Seduction phase (Chapter 10) much easier.

- It reassures her that you are indeed a good catch and are desired by more women than just her.

As with any communication, it is better for her to Observe this situation than to Learn or be Told about it. An example of Observed jealousy can occur if you are on a date and happen to run into another woman; this is particularly effective if this other woman is attractive, affectionate, and clearly the one pursuing you as opposed to vice versa. Since you can't count on this happening, you may have to tell her about a situation if you want her to feel these emotions. If you are on a daytime date, for example, you could mention that you have to be done by 6 p.m. since a friend of yours is coming to cook you dinner. As always, subtlety is key here. She knows that men don't tend to make plans to cook each other dinner, so she'll assume that your friend is a woman, and possibly a rival. Don't say anything more than this. Let her fill in the details.

That being said, nothing can kill a good interaction with a woman as quickly, as totally, and as irreparably as a poorly-executed attempt to induce jealousy. One common mistake is bad timing.

A woman cannot feel jealousy until she is attracted to you. She will also not feel it very intensely until you have qualified her. People fear losing what they have far more than they fear losing what they do not have. Thus, if she feels that she has won you over during the Qualification phase, jealousy will have much more of an impact.

Do not overdo it. Let her imagination do the work for you. "I have to stop off and pick up some wine; a friend is coming over for dinner" is infinitely better than "my hot 21-year old neighbor is so in love with me, she keeps calling wanting to come over; it's really nice." The former sub-communicates value; the latter betrays insecurity. Creating jealousy must always appear accidental. Don't talk about other women unless there's a reason for it.

Respect social norms. If you're on a date, and you run into another woman, it's good to introduce her to your date and talk for a few minutes. It's disrespectful and shows poor Social Intuition to go off with her for 20 minutes and ignore your date. It also shows poor Social Intuition, or implies that you have something to hide, if you brush the other woman off entirely.

Make sure the jealousy is warranted. If you're on a date with a supermodel, bumping into your friend's awkward little sister is unlikely to create much jealousy. A fun little maneuver to increase jealousy is to give an accomplishment introduction for the other woman the same way that you would if you were introducing your wingman into a group (Chapter 21).

Finally, don't ever be jealous yourself. She had a sex life before she met you. If you're attracted to her, other men are too. Get over it. She will mention other men, sometimes in passing, sometimes to test you. Don't ask leading questions (e.g., "did he stay over?") or try to learn more (e.g., "so, this guy you're dating . . ." in an effort to see if she contradicts you over the word 'dating'). Without appearing to be uncomfortable, just change the subject when she talks about other men.

8

IN THIS CHAPTER

Qualification within the model

Why Qualify?

Finding attractive qualities (other than her looks)

Helping her qualify herself

Rewarding her

Qualification within the model

The Qualification phase starts when a woman is attracted to you, and ends when she has attracted you to her. Let's review where Qualification fits into the Emotional Progression Model:

- **Approaching:** Starting a one-topic conversation; neither of you is attracted to the other.

- **Transition:** Starting a normal conversation; neither of you are attracted to the other.

- **Attraction:** She becomes attracted to you or curious about you as a man.

- **Qualification:** You become attracted to her or curious about her as a woman.

- **Comfort:** You build emotional and physical intimacy with each other.

Qualification is the inverse of Attraction. When you were getting a woman's attention during Attraction, she can be said to have been qualifying you. Now, she needs to win your interest, so you qualify her. Put another way, Qualification is when a woman is hitting on you and winning your interest. And you do need to let her win, eventually.

> *Qualification is the first phase in which you should give a woman real compliments.*

Don't get hung up on the apparent linear nature of the Model. It's generally easier to attract a woman before qualifying her, but there can be some overlap. Both Attraction and Qualification levels need to be maintained into the Comfort phase (Chapter 9) and beyond, anyway.

Now, life isn't fair, and one such place in which life is exceedingly not fair is in the differences between the Attraction and the Qualification phases. When you are attracting a woman, she will generally not help you do so. However, when it is her turn to attract you, you will often still have to do much of the work. You may need to prompt her that she still has to win your interest (even though you've already flirting with her), and may even have to help her. And you must do this while making the conversation feel "natural."

Why Qualify?

Qualification can be a counter-intuitive process. After all, you approached a woman because you were interested in her. Why make her win you over once the interaction has already begun?

- The Qualification process gives you reasons to be attracted to her other than her looks. You need these reasons. If you are Pre-selected (see Chapter 3), you wouldn't jump at the first attractive woman who shows interest. And if you only like her for her looks, she'll likely think that you'll leave her when you get what you want or when someone more beautiful comes along.

- Attractive women find it validating but ultimately boring to have men interested in them based on their looks alone.

- Most women enjoy the process of working for the attention of a desirable man. Flirting is a fun game for most women, and she wants to play too.

- If you do not qualify her, she may realize that you were interested in her all along. It's a good thing to be open about your interest in her once you have established sufficient value, but you need her to have earned it. If she realizes that she never did anything to win your interest, her psychology will want her to continue screening you. In contrast, if you've both already screened and won each other over, the Comfort phase can focus on building a connection with each other on a level playing field.

- Qualification solidifies her attraction to you. This relates to the psychological principles of investment and of cognitive dissonance. The more someone invests to gain a result, the more that person wants to achieve it. Cognitive dissonance accounts for most peoples' dislike of holding two contradictory ideas in their head. Thus, if a woman worked hard to win your interest, she will want to believe that your interest was worth winning[5].

---

[5] *These psychological principles can be observed in contexts outside of dating. For example, social fraternities at American universities are notorious for having unpleasant initiation rituals. For someone to voluntarily participate in these rituals, they have to believe that the end result, joining the fraternity, is worth it. Accordingly, those permitted to join will generally feel very strongly about the value of their fraternity.*

Finding Attractive Qualities (other than her looks)

I've said it before, but it's important enough to repeat: her attractive qualities that "win you over" should not be based on her physical appearance. Not even if you think you've seen something new or non-obvious. If she's an attractive woman, she's heard it before.

So what qualities are we looking for? Personally, I think you may as well screen for the same qualities that are genuinely important to you in a woman. This would be a novel idea if you've been buying into influences telling you to do whatever it takes to sleep with any attractive woman who crosses your path. But you bought this book because you're someone who thinks for himself and doesn't follow the herd, so consider giving this approach a try. Figure out what you really want in a woman, and then take this a step further by asking yourself how a woman who possesses those characteristics would present herself. Now, spend your Qualification phase looking for precisely that. For example, among other things I value intelligence and education. I screen for this in Qualification, by asking her about books she has read and movies she has seen.

The more real the qualification process, the less time you will spend with women who do not meet your standards, and the more genuine and welcome your interest will be for the women who do.

Now, if you are only attracted to someone because of her looks or are only interested in a one-night stand, then go ahead and pick some arbitrary characteristics that you can imply you are looking for in a woman. For example, you can ask her about her taste in music, her career or career goals, and her hobbies. She can then "win you over" through what she has to say on these subjects. But still don't make it too easy for her.

Helping her qualify herself

Once you have decided what qualities you are looking for, or are going to appear to be looking for, you need her to convince you that she has them. Surprisingly, many highly-desirable women aren't especially good at this. That's not to say that such women aren't good at seducing men; many are, but these men are usually ones who they see on multiple occasions, at different events connected to their social circle. Even then, many women's strategy is no more sophisticated than going to events where they know that a given man will be present, ensuring that they consistently look good at such events, and taking advantage of opportunities to flirt with him once there. Eventually, he may realize that they are interested in each other.

If you just met her, she probably doesn't know what to do to win your interest. All that most women usually want out of most men who approach them is the validation of knowing that men find them beautiful. Remember, most other men don't have the knowledge or skills that you do from reading this book. Sure, women will occasionally flirt with, date, or hook up with men they just met, but this happens most often when the man is particularly good-looking, high-status, or a "natural" (he naturally employs many of the techniques described in this book), or she is specifically in the mood to meet someone new.

Our techniques are designed to work even when these factors are not present. But this is an unfamiliar situation for many women. Since a woman may not always know what to do to solidify your interest in her, you may need to help.

Qualifiers

A Qualifier is anything that encourages or helps a woman to convey her good qualities to you. A "hard" Qualifier is like a job interview – you make it obvious that you're looking for something, and evaluate what she says accordingly. A "soft" Qualifier should be subtle or imperceptible, making the process feel more "natural." Your Qualifiers should be as soft as possible as long as she is able to demonstrate attractive qualities and feel that she is working for your interest. After all, no one likes job interviews.

A soft Qualifier can be as easy as bringing up topics that are likely to let her express her personality and give you reasons to be attracted to her. Examples include:

- Travel.

- Career.

- Education.

- Hobbies.

- Pets.

- Cooking.

- What-if questions ("if you could be any animal, what would you be?" etc.).

Any of these can be introduced as a question or a statement. With travel, for example, you can ask "Do you like to travel?" and follow up with questions like "where have you been?" "where did you like most?" or "where do you most want to go?" Don't ask all of these, of course, or she'll feel like she's being interviewed. Using statements, you can say something like, "I love to travel" and wait for her reaction. If she is attracted to you, she will want to talk about interests you have in common.

Mix statements and questions. Don't rely only on one or the other.

You can make the Qualifier a bit harder by asking her open-ended questions about herself such as "so, what's your story?" or "so who are you?" or "and you are...?" When she starts to talk, use clarifying questions and your own anecdotes to guide her into revealing positive qualities. I prefer these types of Qualifiers for a couple of reasons. First, you can find out a lot more about someone than if you direct the conversation to a specific topic, like one of the topics listed above. Second, this approach requires her to think. If I'm interested in a woman, I don't want her to get through the Qualification phase with responses that she might be able to give off the top of her head. The extra investment on her part strengthens her connection to me.

The hardest Qualifiers risk coming across as arrogant or socially awkward. However, they can be useful when you feel a woman is interested in you but needs to work harder. This could happen if, for example, I meet a very physically attractive woman at a trendy nightclub who is excitable and in "party mode." I would assume that a woman with her looks, personality and social habits meets and flirts with a lot of men. One way to make sure I stand out (especially if we're not going to leave together and I'll have to follow up with a phone call) is to get her deeply invested in the process of qualifying herself.

Here are a couple of very hard Qualifiers:

- So what do you have going for you?

- Why should I take your number / call you / be interested in you?

Some women will naturally and easily address the hardest Qualifiers. Others take a bit of coaxing and warming up. It's a good practice to start the Qualification phase with something softer first, to get her used to the idea of trying to win your approval, and doing so through her personality instead of her looks.

Rewarding her

Reward a woman when she tells you something about herself that makes you more interested in her.

After all, this is what we want her to be doing. Compliments make good rewards. But they must feel authentic. Show that the subject is genuinely important to you by talking about it. For example, if she says she loves sailing, compliment her and then talk about a time when you went sailing, or why you'd like to learn. This is where Qualification leads into Comfort, as you can use her responses to your Qualifiers as a catalyst to explore commonalities.

You can and should reward her if she makes a genuine effort to address a harder Qualifier, even if she fails to give much of answer. Keep in mind that it can be tough to be put on the spot like this, especially in a high-energy social environment like a nightclub. If she's trying, be nice to her, switch to another subject, and try a softer Qualifier in a minute. Her putting in the effort is what is important.

However, you don't want to make it too easy. In the same way that a desirable woman is not likely to be deeply interested in you based on one aspect of your personality, you should not be won over after learning just one attractive thing about her. You'll want to qualify her on a few different subjects.

Take your time and space these out. Weave some general conversation between Qualifiers. The more natural this feels, the better. Women won't take you seriously if they don't feel you are sincere, or if they get the impression that you are working off of a checklist.

So a successful Qualification process should look something like this:

1. Qualifier

2. Her response

3. Explore the topic

4. Compliment

5. Pull back (optional)

6. New topic

7. Next Qualifier

Pulling Back

What does pulling back mean? Too many compliments can make her feel uncomfortable, lessen her feeling that you're a challenge, or put her back into the frame that she is screening you. A pullback cuts the compliment off and changes the frame of the conversation away from you expressing interest in her.

Pullbacks should be light and playful. Your pullback should never imply anything seriously negative about her, though it can include some mildly dismissive body language (e.g., turning slightly away). Most of the time they start with "too bad you are" followed by some childlike teasing. "Too bad you're such a dork" is a classic. I also like to use characteristics that are true but can't possibly be reasons why I wouldn't be interested in her. For example:

- Too bad you come to [wherever you both are].

- Too bad about our age difference [if we're about the same age].

- Too bad you are [astrological sign].

- Too bad I don't like you [smiling and playful tonality are especially important here].

When she has done enough work to win you over, let her know. Give her an overall compliment, as opposed to one based on one specific element of her personality. Or just come out and tell her you are interested in her or curious about her. Make such a statement consistent with how you've been interacting with her up until this point. For example, if you've previously been teasing her, such a statement could be: "you know, I wasn't really sure about you when I first met you, but we've got a lot in common. Cool." Or the simpler "you are amazing." Now you're in the Comfort phase.

Sample one-subject qualification

I have deliberately made the woman in this example more difficult than most, to help illustrate the process. Anything in square brackets [like this] represents things that I wouldn't actually say, but can help guide you through my thought process. Assume that I have already Approached, Transitioned, and Attracted this woman.

Me: So, what's your story?

Her: What do you mean?

Me: Tell me about yourself. [Sometimes, "what's your story" doesn't work. No big deal. Just rephrase it. You could also say "What do you do for fun?" if you sense that she's not willing or able to deal with unstructured questions. Or go to a softer Qualifier.]

Her: Well, I'm a photographer, I like to dance, I work in a gallery... [None of these three things seem to lead easily to anything that I am attracted to. So I will use her interest in photography to explore other aspects of her personality.]

Me: Photography. Really? You don't seem like someone who would be interested in photography... that's cool... I like taking pictures because I travel so much. I have a couple of shots that I took when I was camping and whitewater rafting in Colorado last year that make me really happy when I look at them. [I've given her a hint of a reward by saying "that's cool." On the other hand, since I don't actually care about hotography, I've given her four potential conversation-starters here: travel, Colorado, camping, and whitewater rafting. If she is interested in any of these, then we have something in common that is important to me, and this could give me one reason to be interested in her. If she ignores all four of these and sticks with photography, then at least I'm talking about how photography makes me feel as opposed to the technical details. Feelings are always better than facts for making a connection. Notice, by the way, that I'm still throwing DHVs into the conversation where appropriate in order to maintain attraction levels, even after the Attraction phase is over.]

Her: Yeah, I have one from this trip to New York that I really love; it's of the sun setting behind the Empire State Building. [It looks like we might

Me: It's amazing how you notice little things more when you're traveling, isn't it? Her: Yeah, for sure.

Me: I love to travel. Especially in Europe. I want to go to Australia. [Everyone likes traveling in Europe and Australia. This is a safe bet. Obviously, modify this if you are currently in Europe or Australia.]

Her: Me too!

Me: [Now I'm getting somewhere.] Really? I always seem to get along better with people who are adventurous and curious and want to get out and see the world. [Notice how she has started to win my approval.] Some friends of mine just got back from Australia and they said it's so beautiful... great beaches... great diving... good hiking... really interesting cities with lots to do. I have a friend who just opened this super-hot restaurant in Sydney and I'm going to go visit him soon [DHV].

Her: That sounds fun. I want to go snorkeling and see that big coral reef.

Me: That's awesome! [She's winning more of my approval now.] I've always wanted to learn to dive, and I just got my certification. Ever since I was a kid I used to watch those nature shows on the oceans and always thought that stuff was so beautiful.

Chapter 9: Comfort

9

IN THIS CHAPTER:

What is Comfort?

You enter the Comfort phase as soon as you finish the Qualification phase. This is where you usually:

- Build an emotional connection and get to know each other.

- Tone down any dismissive attitude from previous phases.

- Solidify and sustain attraction and qualification levels.

- Increase physical intimacy (touching) with appropriate pacing: neither too fast or too slow.

- Get her phone number and go on dates if appropriate.

- Manage the whole process so that she feels genuinely comfortable being in a sexual situation with you.

The last of these – comfort in a sexual situation – represents the end point of the Comfort phase. A sexual situation is one in which a woman is engaging in sexual behavior (touching that goes beyond kissing) in a place where sex could realistically happen. When you have established that level of comfort together, you have finished Comfort and entered Seduction. (Just in case there is any confusion – this is not to imply that you should stop making her feel comfortable when in Seduction or that the only purpose of building comfort is to get her ready for sex).

While some women can reach this level of comfort quite easily, given the right man and the right situation, most women present more of a challenge. Indeed, some follow "rules" like the Third Date Rule or the One Month Rule to govern their sexual behavior. A woman who follows such rules will be less likely to make a sexual decision "in the moment" that she may later regret. Sleeping with too many people, or sleeping with someone "too early" carries greater consequences for women than for men. We examine the impact of these consequences in the following chapter, on Seduction.

The good news about these rules is that you do not need to directly challenge them. All you have to do is solve the underlying comfort issues. Your interest is to move quickly through the Comfort phase because there are many variables in a woman's life that you cannot control. Women become busy or meet other men all the time. The more comfort you have built in the time available to you, the greater the chance that she will see you as a priority in her life and see you again. If you moved too slowly, you may get lost in the shuffle.

Still, the Comfort phase will usually take at least a couple hours. Most women need this time to build a feeling of mutual connection. It also allows her to see whether you remain congruent with the way in which you initially presented yourself. Women do this to avoid being deceived or sleeping with someone based on an inaccurate first impression.

Not all time is equal. You build more of a connection with a woman the more you see her over a shorter period of time. Seeing her once a week builds more comfort than once a month, even if you spend the same total amount of time with her. Seeing her more frequently, even for shorter periods of time, has the additional benefit of helping with women who follow rules like the Third Date Rule.

Of course, proper application of the techniques in this chapter should usually get you through the Comfort phase in the first or second (or occasionally the third) meeting.

That being said, the whole concept of seeing her repeatedly implies some sharing of contact information and arranging future plans. We cover this process in extensive detail in Chapters 16 (Dates) and 22 (Phone Game). In this chapter, we talk about the process and the end goal of Comfort, as well as how to build comfort in the first meeting.

The Basic Comfort List

Maximize the value of your time together. The Basic Comfort List below goes over some of the more universal activities and processes that help in doing so:

Basic Comfort List

- Learning about each others' life, job, friends, hobbies, family, etc.

- Finding commonalities: similar interests, similar experiences.

- Discovering shared values.

- Sharing vulnerabilities.

- Winning peer approval (her friends and/or family like you).

- Doing activities together.

- Making future plans.

- Projecting future adventures (more complex; discussed below).

- Leading her through a range of emotions, including some strong ones.

- Being trustworthy, especially in situations in which she has to rely on her trust in you (e.g., being in your house alone with you).

- Not pressuring her for sex.

Some items on this list probably feel very familiar. You have likely seen men – men who do not have access to the type of material revealed in Magic Bullets – start conversations with women with questions like "what do you do?" and "where are you from?" While this is usually painful to watch, I understand what they are trying to do: they are attempting to learn about a given woman's life and are hoping to find commonalities. They are doing the right kind of thing, but at the wrong time. Building comfort does not interest most women until and unless a man has already created attraction (Attraction phase) and a sense of a challenge (Qualification phase).

It is vitally important to build comfort during your first interaction with a woman: the one in which you Open, Transition, Attract, and Qualify her. If you do not do so, your odds of seeing her again are pretty low, even if you do get her phone number or arrange a date. See Chapter 22 on Phone Game for a detailed explanation of why this is. The major exception to this rule is if there is some external reason why you will meet again, like if you are both always at the gym at the same time. This is more of a Social Circle type of situation (Chapter 12).

You have two major hurdles to building Comfort during your first interaction:

- When you initially meet a woman, she will usually be with a group of people. It can be difficult to build comfort between two virtual strangers when other people are around, observing or participating in the conversation.

- You might be constrained by the social situation in which you find yourself, either in terms of the amount of time available to you or in terms of the appropriateness of different activities. Unfortunately, some items on the Basic Comfort List are not useful in your first interaction with a woman.

We will deal with each of these hurdles (Comfort and Group Dynamics in the First Meeting & Comfort and Logistics in the First Meeting) in turn.

Comfort and Group Dynamics in the First Meeting

Solving the first of these challenges generally requires you to create a situation whereby you can have a private conversation with her, away from her friends. This is not a cultish attempt to deprive her of her peer network; such a conversation will be temporary and usually where her friends can see you. It is simply a mechanism for getting to know each other on the kind of personal level that is much more difficult if other people are present.

The easiest way to engender a private conversation is to start slowly, and only move her a few feet away. For example, you might motion for her to move slightly to the side as if you wanted to show her something or she were in someone else's way. Then you might move between her and her group. Now you're in a private conversation. You can accomplish the same thing by slowly moving in a certain direction during your conversation and motioning for her to follow you.

When you want to move her further away, for example to an empty table, it's important to have a pretext. Saying "let's talk in private" can feel socially awkward and almost sinister, as well as unnecessarily exclusionary to her group. The actual pretext is not very important, and there are thousands of possibilities, such as:

- Going inside or outside where it is cooler or warmer.

- Going somewhere quieter so you can hear each other.

- Going where you can show her some pictures from your camera.

- Going to meet your friends.

- Going where you can tell her a long and involved story.

- Going over to the bar to get a drink.

Obviously, not all of these will be appropriate in every situation.

Don't try to move her too far from her friends, at least at first, as this might make her feel uncomfortable. Her friends will want to make sure that she is safe and that she is having a good time. Make the first move to somewhere where her friends can see her. Later, you can move her to somewhere more private, for example to kiss her (see Chapter 19).

When you move her, it's important to implicitly acknowledge her and her group's potential concerns, but don't abandon your dominant frame. In other words, deal with potential objections without making the private conversation a big deal. Two examples should serve to illustrate this point:

- Point at a nearby empty table that is in easy view of the group and tell her: "come with me to that table over there and I'll show you that video clip on my cell phone.

- Say to her group "Do you guys mind if I borrow your friend for a few minutes? We'll be right over there and we'll leave a few chairs empty for you if you want to join us in a few moments." (This example also has the added benefit of presupposing that she will come with you.)

If you act as if something is a big deal, it will become one. Don't say something silly like "I know you'd be worried about your friend. Don't be worried. I'm only taking her over to that table. I'm harmless, see? If you want to come over every few minutes and check up on her, that's ok." You will not only come off as weak and submissive, but you will also fail to accomplish anything, since now you've made her safety a central issue. On the other hand, saying "follow me somewhere else" sounds ominous and will make people think about where you are taking her and why.

Starting private conversations is vastly easier if you have a friend (wingman) out with you. We discuss this in Chapter 21 on "Winging."

Alternatives to Isolation

Most men who are experts with women, including most Love Systems instructors, actively try to create the circumstances for private conversations. They are very successful at doing so and enjoy excellent results. While I also do this, I also let these conversations come about naturally or induce them subtly, and have developed a series of techniques to make this happen.

One of my good friends suggests that I call it the lazy method. It's true. I'm quite lazy sometimes. I still have a $50 coupon to The Gap from a year ago that I'm too lazy to go to the mall and use. (Plus, I hate their clothes.) Starting private conversations takes work, and managing them takes work too. I like meeting lots of people, especially when I can just hang out. When I go out, I'll see Love Systems' instructors like Braddock, Cajun, The Don, Sheriff, Mr. M, or Tenmagnet in various parts of a bar, making out with various beautiful women and it's great to see. I'm usually in the same group the whole night. We all usually end up going home or making plans with beautiful women at the end of the night, but I like my way because it's a lot less work. So, yes, I can be lazy. Now I've admitted it to the world.

One caveat: while this works for me and a small number of others, it has not been tested by large numbers of people in different situations. This is in contrast to the strategies to actively create private conversations from the previous section. Treat this approach as experimental. If you are curious to try something new, go for it and let me know how it works. If not, our standard methodology will serve you very well. As always, no one single theory is a magic bullet for success with women, which is why we present multiple options in situations like these.

In one sentence:

> *This approach relies on winning the approval of a woman's group to create opportunities for spontaneous isolation and for deep comfort-building even within a group setting.*

Peer Group Approval

Winning the approval of her group (neutrality can be enough to make this approach work, but peer group approval is what allows it to be so powerful) does not happen by chance. I pro-actively find ways to bring value to her friends, through such things as making them laugh, talking about their areas of interest and expertise, or implying that I will introduce them to people they would like to meet. For example, to a single man in a group, I might talk about a female friend who might be joining me later who I'd love to introduce him to, because he seems "cool" based on specific qualities, which I mention, that I've noticed about him. You can nearly always bond with men over sports, cars, or certain television shows or movies. You can bond with most women over popular culture, fashion, celebrity gossip, or by using a toned-down version of the techniques from earlier chapters of this book.

Once there is mutual attraction and some comfort with a woman I'm interested in, I usually look for an opportunity to state my interest in her to her friends. I don't want to do this right in front of her, so I'll wait until she goes to the restroom or to get a drink or is otherwise removed from the conversation. I will usually say something like "So tell me about [woman's name]?" or "[Woman's name] seems pretty interesting; what's the catch?" This makes my interest in her unambiguous.

What happens next is very important. If her friends tell me good things about her, it is as if they are encouraging me to pursue her. By doing so in a conversation in which she is not present, they become somewhat complicit in the developing courtship, as long as she remains interested in me. It would not be psychologically consistent to see their friend interested in me, to encourage me to pursue her by telling me good things about her, and then discourage us from getting to know each other later.

The downside risk of making my interest explicit to her friends at this stage is very small. By the time I am in Comfort, her friends will know that I am interested in her anyway. I am also sure to find out how they all know each other early on in the interaction, to be able to assess the situation. If people in her group do object to my interest and I have somehow not noticed this up to this point, then I would rather learn about this sooner than later. Perhaps one of her friends objects to me on grounds that I can deal with (e.g., "no, that wasn't me kissing the brunette by the bar"), in which case it's better to address the issue than to leave him as an unknown but hostile element within the group. Or, if I can't deal with a friend's objections – usually a frustrated orbiter who wants her for himself – at least I know about them and can plan my strategy for the rest of the night accordingly. Usually, however, a single woman's friends will be encouraging. Obviously, this will not work if the woman is not single (unless her friends don't care). I tend to focus on single women, but if you don't feel this way, you're better off trying to create private conversations… and get a bodyguard.

Spontaneous Isolation

Social groups do not usually stay perfectly still over the course of the night. People go the bathroom, they get drinks, they dance, they look for their friends, they get more drinks, they go to have a cigarette, and they do dozens of other things that entail moving. (Not everyone is as lazy as I am.) Any time this happens is an opportunity for me to be in isolation with the woman I'm interested in, since she will always have a choice between going with her friends and waiting for them to come back.

Her friends' approval of me is important because it will govern how they frame this choice. If they don't like me, they won't make the situation sound like a choice at all. For example, they may say "Come on, we need a drink, let's go." Of course, she still has a choice, and women can and do tell their friends in these situations to go ahead without them and that they will wait for them to come back, but this is awkward and requires a woman to be deeply attracted and to have a strong personality.

In contrast, if her friends do like me, they may instead say something like "we're going to get a drink, do you want to come or do you want to wait for us here?" or even "we're going to get a drink, do you want anything?" They may also do this even if they are neutral toward me, but she has already indicated to them that she is interested in me, either explicitly or through focusing the conversation on her and me. One caveat: if a woman appears to be all over a man, especially if she's drunk, her friends may not want to leave her alone with him.

Deep Comfort in a group setting

Even if her friends don't or can't leave her, this should not hold me back. Once I already have some comfort with her and have befriended her friends, my favorite position in which to advance the relationship in a group setting is to have my arm around her or have her curled into me (depending on everyone's comfort level), while I primarily address conversation to her friends. I can still focus the conversation on comfort-building topics and allow her to get to know me; after all, she will still be listening and interjecting. In this situation, I build comfort both by what I am saying and by demonstrating that I get along with her friends and that they approve of me.

Of course, this scenario does not provide obvious opportunities to allow her to "open up" to me in intimate personal conversation if her friends are all listening. However, conversations in groups of four or more people tend to ebb and flow, sometimes breaking apart into several side conversations and sometimes coming together to one conversation in which everyone participates. At some point there will be an opportunity for me to have a private conversation with her when her friends are all talking to each other. It is a rare circumstance in which her friends never leave, even temporarily, and never allow a side conversation. If this happens, and I am alone and I need a private conversation with her, then I will get over my laziness and induce one.

Usually, of course, I will have friends with me who can help. Or on Love Systems' workshops, I will have some of the top men in the world: men like The Don, Sheriff, Tenmagnet, Mr. M, Braddock, and others. They can easily engage her friends, and I do the same for them.

If I don't happen to have friends available to help, and opportunities for an intimate conversation aren't coming with this as quickly as I would like, and for whatever reason I don't want to try to induce a private conversation, then I can improvise with some more advanced tactics, such as involving her friends in conversation with nearby attractive people of the opposite sex.

For example, let's say I approached, transitioned, attracted, and qualified a woman who is at a restaurant with two male friends. During Comfort, we might all be sitting together. As soon as I see two attractive women nearby, I will shift the conversation to an opinion opener. I won't run it as an opener, of course, but I will bring up the topic and create discussion. Within 30-60 seconds, I can then say "let's get another opinion" and engage the two women in this conversation. From that point, it's simply a matter of leading the group to a normal conversation, with no need to create attraction, and gradually letting the two men take over. If they have chemistry, the large group conversation should then break into many smaller conversations. At this point, the woman I'm interested in will be impressed with my Social Intuition and her friends will love me for setting them up. Moreover, they will likely not be at all worried about what I'm doing with their friend; they will probably be grateful that I'm keeping her out of their way!

Quick Comfort

Whichever approach you use to deal with a woman's group dynamics, some comfort-building activities require more time or different logistics than you are likely to have the first time you meet someone. For example, it may be midnight and you, your friends, and her friends are all at the restaurant where you met a few hours ago. The two of you are not likely to run off and shop together for a picnic in the park, no matter how much comfort this would build.

Therefore, it is highly advisable to modify comfort-building techniques and dating ideas to first-meeting situations. Here are some of my favorites:

- Get to another venue (even if you take all her friends). You instantly go from being "the guy I met at Restaurant X" to "the guy we are hanging out with." If you met her and her group at a coffee shop, you can invite them to the mall, or to dinner. If you met at a restaurant, you can go to a bar for a drink or to a dessert place. If you met at a bar or nightclub, you can go to a different bar or nightclub, or to a late-night restaurant, or to an after-party. Oversell where you are going, but make sure it's at least moderately fun. Have a positive reason for going somewhere. Also, make it seem like somewhere you are going anyway. Combining all three of these elements could make such an invitation sound like this: "Hey, we were just on our way to Café Gideon, they have the best music and the best drinks ever... have you ever been? No? You HAVE to go. Anyway, some of my very good friends are there, really great people. I'd love to introduce you. You guys should come along for a little bit and check it out." Then act like they said yes, continue the conversation normally, and get ready to go there.

- Use specific conversational tactics to direct the conversation toward personal intimacy and secrets, as you may not have enough one-on-one time to get there for the conversation to get there naturally. I recommend using the technique known as the question game. Performed only in isolation other people can be there, as in the Whole Group Method, but they can't be listening, the point is to ask each other questions, back and forth, about very personal subjects.

- This clearly will lead to sharing secrets, learning about each other, and heightening the sexual element of your conversation; however, it will usually sound contrived to most women. Thus, we present it as a "game" with somewhat arbitrary rules such as "you can only ask questions in ten words or less" or "you can't ask questions that have already been asked." I also do not let a woman ask questions – at least initially – questions such as "how many brothers do you have" or "what is your favorite food?" There is no point playing a game to share this sort of information; it can be done in the presence of a larger group. I prefer to set the tone for these sorts of games with very personal questions such as "have you ever kissed your friend's boyfriend?"; "what were you like in high school?"; or "what's the one thing you'd least want your parents to know about you?". Check out the Love Systems Routines Manual under: [www.LoveSystems.com/Routines] for a fuller treatment of the question game and similar routines.

The question game provides a great opportunity to kiss her. See Chapter 19.

- Future plans can build comfort. These are often kept vague. When you and a woman realize you have an interest in common, you can suggest specific plans but without necessarily including a specific timeframe or making firm plans. For example, if you and she have a shared interest in art museums, you can say "oh, we should go check out the Cezanne exhibit at the National Gallery." You can add "next weekend" onto the end of this, but don't try to turn it into a date, unless she does. If you create a few future plans like this, she may start to think of you as a potential continuing presence in her life. You can also frame future plans as activities you are going to do anyway. For example: "I'm going to check out the Cezanne exhibit at the National Gallery next weekend; you're welcome to come along." This places you more in the role of the leader, and is useful for Breakthrough Comfort (see below). However, you will have to deal with small hurdles if she does want to join you, since you will have to bring your friends or she may wonder why they cancelled on you and whether you really did have plans to do something like you said. If you say that you planned to go alone, this might also appear odd. These hurdles are all extremely minor and solvable; I list them here only so you can keep them in mind.

- Future projections are closely related to this. Future projections are related to future plans but with a time shift. Instead of talking about what you will do together, you talk about what you will have done. For example, you could talk about what you and she will do after you have spent the next six months seeing every gallery in the city. Describe the emotions and events that you both will encounter on this journey – all in a somewhat playful and not serious tone, but in the past tense, so she imagines knowing you for six months and having these adventures with you. Imagining herself being closer to you at some point in the future will often make her feel closer to you in the present moment.

- You can also build comfort through the use of conspiracy and inside jokes. Giving her a nickname early on in the Attraction phase, and then calling it back can build comfort. As can making comments about other people outside of her group in the bar or club. Anything you can do to establish an "us vs. the world" dynamic is massively helpful.

Breakthrough Comfort

Breakthrough Comfort describes the advanced comfort-building processes first publicized by former Love Systems' instructors Sinn and Future in January 2007. Start by mastering the techniques from the Basic Comfort List above, as well as learning to smoothly get phone numbers, practice phone game, and go on dates (see Chapter 22). When you're enjoying consistent success, try some of the elements of Breakthrough Comfort for major acceleration:

- Show your passion and purpose. You must be able to convey to her convincingly that you are a man of a greater purpose. Set the frame that you are going places where she will want to be and that you are driven to pursue your life goals and do so without any hesitation. Be specific as to what you want your life to be defined by and what you are doing to accomplish it.

- See her passion and purpose. Most women have a purpose that they secretly strive to achieve. Learn what it is. You need this to compliment her deeply and to relate your worlds to each other (the following two elements). You must be able to find out her core value, the reason that she is pursuing the life path she is on.

- Compliment deeply... then release. Use your knowledge of her passion and purpose to compliment her intensely on her qualities that will help her achieve them. This communicates that you see her as the woman that the little girl inside her yearns to be. Add small (I stress small) releases at the end to avoid deep compliments from "hanging" in the conversation and creating potential awkwardness. For example: "You are absolutely amazing and whatever you want to be I can see you doing that because of X, Y, and Z. Too bad you're a bit of a dork." The release is there to avoid awkwardness, but it is small enough that you do not take away her validation from the compliment.

- Relate your worlds to each other, and to the greatness of your passion and purpose. You want her to have the feeling that both of you are bound for greatness and are on the same general path, even if in different fields. You just happen to be further along, but can nudge her in the right direction, in the same way as someone did for you earlier.

- Make your vague plans real. In Breakthrough Comfort, your credibility is both crucial and extremely sensitive. Use the alternative approach to future plans – where you say that you are going to do something, and she can come along. In Breakthrough Comfort, you must ensure that these plans must actually happen when you say that they will (at least for you, if the woman in question does not join you) in order to support your credibility in other elements of your interaction with her. This extends to the things you are doing without her.

- Create the feeling of a "whirlwind courtship." Breakthrough Comfort works best the more you see her over a shorter period of time. See her every day or every couple days or call her more than once in a day. For this reason, Breakthrough Comfort is best suited if you want to pursue some kind of long-term relationship with a woman. Otherwise, you may leave her hurt or resentful. This approach can make you seem needy if not pursued in the right frame, which is one reason why Breakthrough Comfort is an advanced tactic.

Even with all of these tools at your disposal, building comfort is not as easy as it looks. This is because you have other processes to manage at the same time while you are in the Comfort phase. The two most important of these are: sustaining attraction and qualification levels, and increasing physical intimacy (touching).

Sustaining attraction and qualification

It's in the nature of things for the excitement, interest, and tension you built during the Attraction and the Qualification phases to dissipate over time. Even while building comfort, make sure you periodically refresh her attraction to you and re-introduce the "screening" frame from Qualification. If you do not, you risk losing your sex appeal to her and being put in the dreaded Let's-Just-Be-Friends Zone (LJBF). Qualification even extends to the Relationship phase, as women need to constantly be reassured as to why you like them.

Many women get great psychological satisfaction from having men in their social circle who consistently desire them. We call these men "orbiters". In addition to friendship, these men provide attention, protection, companionship, and ego-validation. If a woman realizes that she can sustain your interest for a long period of time without letting you develop the relationship, she might be tempted to LJBF you. We discussed above why you don't want to try to push a woman too quickly through Comfort. The LJBF Zone is why you don't want to push her too slowly either.

10

Seduction within the model

What we call the Seduction phase begins when she is comfortable enough to engage in sexual behavior (beyond kissing) with you, in a place where sex could realistically happen. Both elements are important here. No matter how sexual you are both being, if you're out in public, you're not in Seduction... unless you are both exhibitionists. Or if she's in your bedroom but won't let anything happen other than kissing, you're still in Comfort.

The Seduction phase ends the first time you have sex. If you want there to be a second time, you move to the Relationship phase. As you will see, "relationship" refers to the context for ongoing sexual encounters and does not necessarily imply commitment or monogamy.

All of this makes Seduction one of the more straightforward phases to understand. You start when she is ready to engage you sexually, and end when you have sex with her.

Why women (sometimes) resist sex

The good news here is that Seduction is not usually where most men have their biggest problems. If you've done a good job in Attraction, Qualification, and Comfort and you're not in a rush, then you will usually succeed at this one eventually. Women want and enjoy sex as much as men. Sexual arousal (as opposed to sexual decision-making) happens as quickly for women as it does for men[6].

The bad news is that, from a logical perspective, she probably shouldn't have sex with you. Nothing personal, but you're a new man. Sex with someone new might make her feel that she is easy or make her emotionally vulnerable or scare her that things are moving too far in case you're not right for her. She also risks your losing interest because she let things move too fast, or your telling her friends. All of this comes in addition to risking pregnancy or disease.

It can be difficult for a woman to admit, even to herself, that she wants to add a new name to the list of men she's slept with. Society tends to be pretty judgmental about female sexual behavior and few women want to be thought of – by them-

---

[6] *There is a fascinating and detailed study of this in The Journal of Sexual Medicine, January 2007 if you're interested in further reading.*

selves or others – as "easy" or a "slut" or "whore." This isn't something easy for men to relate to. There are no male equivalents for these words or for the societal judgments that give them such power. Yes, some women are very comfortable and confident with their sexuality and sexual decision-making. These women are often great catches, but are not the majority.

The Seduction phase is a woman's last chance to "speak now or forever hold her peace." There are two consequences to this. First, lingering issues from previous phases will often surface here. For example, if you're in bed with her and she asks "Why do you like me?" or "Am I just another girl to you?" it may mean that you did an incomplete job of guiding her through the necessary emotions for her to feel special to you. Likely, you didn't give her the feeling that she won your interest through unique aspects of her personality in the Qualification phase and/or you did not connect deeply with her in the Comfort phase. You can fix some of these kinds of issues when in Seduction, but it's not ideal to have to do so. Second, your margin for error is smaller. A woman may give you a "free pass" with a bad Opener, because all she risks is that you'll bore her for a couple of minutes in a Transition or in Attraction. She's not going to give you a free pass in Seduction, where the stakes are higher.

Alright, enough talking about seduction. Let's go over how to do it.

Pacing

Make the journey feel natural.

A good analogy for Seduction done properly is being on a car trip where you were enjoying the ride and talking to your friend in the driver's seat, and weren't consciously thinking about being on a journey until you arrived at your destination. This is how Seduction should feel for a woman.

The key element here is to avoid jarring interruptions. If the driver had stopped to ask for directions, appeared nervous about the trip, started acting differently all of sudden, drove too fast or too slow, or did anything dangerous, you would fall out of your comfort zone. Your mental pattern switches from enjoying your friend's company to focusing on the journey. You'll start thinking about what is going on, and how, and why.

This is not helpful for you because it tends to focus a woman's logical mind on whether she should have sex. As we just saw in the previous section, there are many reasons for her to say no. In addition, many women find it a turnoff to have to actively participate in their own seduction. Consider romance novels, which are pretty much entirely directed at women. He wants her, she's reluctant, he wants her more, she accedes, and then finally they couple up in a fit of passion. He takes 100% of the responsibility for leading her to sex in a way that is exciting and comfortable for her.

In a sexual context, we use the term "state break" to describe the jarring interruptions that force a woman to logically and consciously address whether she is on the road to having sex with you. Examples of state breaks include: coming home with you, taking off clothes or talking about sex, or getting a condom.

Our best tools to deal with state breaks are avoidance, blurring, and distraction. This leads us to the "ABD model of seduction."

Avoidance bypasses the state break altogether. In the driving analogy, planning your route to avoid red lights or adjusting your speed so that the light isn't red by the time you hit the intersection are examples of avoidance.

Blurring reduces the intensity of the state break. You minimize the state break by mixing the old, comfortable activity with the new, potential uncomfortable, activity. For a red light, this means putting on the breaks to come to a very gradual stop at the intersection instead of slamming them at the last second.

Distraction does not attempt to mitigate the state break but introduces something new that is an even stronger stimulus so she focuses on that instead. For example, if you turn up the volume on her favorite song playing on the radio or point out a celebrity in the next lane, this may distract her from the state break of hitting the red light.

As a final note in this section, I want to be clear that when I talk about minimizing jarring interruptions that force her to engage her logical mind, this is not the same as hypnotizing or befuddling her so she's not capable of making a rational decision. Sex has to be consensual, and that consent has to be meaningful.

Let's proceed with some examples on how to use avoidance, blurring, and distraction to deal with major state breaks in Seduction:

State Break #1: Bringing her home

Avoidance: Don't get sexual until you get home. There is no point. In fact, if you try to arouse her before you try to get her to your house, she will know what your agenda is. You may not even get another date if she thinks that a successful date with you has to end in sex.

Avoidance: Plan to do activities in or near your house. It's much easier to get into Seduction if the two of you are already in your living room or around the corner than if you're in two separate cars at the other end of town. This is a great strategy for dates (Chapter 16).

Avoidance: Don't ask her if she'd like to come home with you. Lead her home. Hold her hand and walk her to your car. Don't ask; assume that she's getting in. Don't volunteer that you're taking her home.

Avoidance: Make her comfortable being in your house well before you're in the Seduction phase. If she's learned that she's safe and can have fun in private with you during Comfort without your trying to sleep with her, taking her home in the future will be less likely to induce a state break.

Blurring: Bring her home for a reason other than to have sex with her. Saying to a woman "would you like to come back to my house" will often be interpreted as an invitation to have sex. You can blur this a bit by inviting her home to check out your photographs, or to lend her a book, or whatever. You can blur it even more by being out with her in your neighborhood and leading her to your house "for a second" while you get your wallet or use the bathroom.

Distraction: Say you are leaving a party with a woman. You each live 20 minutes away, in opposite directions. Bringing her home will be a state break that is tough to avoid or blur. So distract her. Use avoidance or blurring to get her into your car and then don't stop talking. Tell her interesting stories to engage her logical mind so she's not left alone with her thoughts. You can go through extended monologues to entertain and distract women's logical mind at moments that would otherwise be sure to cause a state break, like waiting in line to check into a hotel.

State Break #2: Moving her to the bedroom

Avoidance: Use your living room couch the first time you have sex with her, or at least until she is sufficiently aroused (distraction) that the state break doesn't hurt you. Or put something non-sexual and interesting to do in the bedroom so it's not a state break to be in there and so you won't have to move her later.

Blurring: Same idea as in the "bringing her home" state break above.

Distraction: Arousal is a good all-purpose distraction. Most people will ignore some of the less important interruptions from their logical brains if they are turned on enough. Picking a woman up and carrying her into the bedroom is another distraction technique, and may arouse her at the same time.

State Break #3: Removing clothes

Avoidance: Don't remove anything that isn't necessary. If she's wearing a skirt, you don't need to remove anything at all. This causes fewer state breaks. If you enjoy the process of undressing a woman, save it for the second time you sleep with her if you anticipate any resistance the first time.

Blurring: Don't suddenly move from one sexual activity to another. Say you're touching her breasts and she's comfortable with that but not with you touching her genitals. Don't suddenly shift all of your attention from above to below her waist. Keep touching her breasts but also touch closer and closer to her genitals without stopping what you are doing with her chest. As long as she remains comfortable, you can steadily intensify your sexual touching this way.

Distraction: Once you're home, distraction is usually physical. An excellent time to remove clothes is when she is getting a lot of physical pleasure from you, by doing anything from kissing her neck to oral sex.

Bonus: This doesn't really fit in any of the three categories, but I'm not going to hide good information to make the model seem more elegant. Every man knows – or should know – that when you remove a woman's skirt or pants, take her underwear off at the same time in the same motion (i.e., grab both). If you leave her underwear on, taking it off later is a major state break.

State Break #4: Condoms

Avoidance: Uh, no. It's not that uncommon for a woman to be completely willing to have unprotected sex with you while aroused and "in the moment" but to have a state break triggered by your getting a condom. You don't need a safe sex warning, but it's amazing how many guys will skip the condom to avoid the state break. Plan for this scenario, and Blur or Distract instead (see below).

Blurring: Avoid this problem by keeping condoms near the bed, where you can get to them easily and unobtrusively. Or keep one in the pocket of your pants, and remember when you take your pants off not to throw them too far out of reach.

Distraction: Performing oral sex is an excellent time to put a condom on. After she has an orgasm or has had enough, she will inevitably pull you up to kiss her or to have her face near yours. If you have a condom on, penetration should follow naturally, especially with the added lubrication from oral sex.

State Break #5: Penetration

<u>Avoidance:</u> Why? You must have the wrong book.

<u>Blurring:</u> With a condom on, you have a lot of freedom for rubbing, "teasing," and otherwise intensifying genital-genital contact (usually while kissing her lips or neck, sometimes ears). If she questions this, tell her you believe in safety even for just rubbing up together. She'll know that this isn't the full story, but it should satisfy her logical mind. At that point, arousal and increased wetness can make penetrative sex "just happen."

<u>Distraction:</u> If you come up with a way to distract a woman from the fact that you are having sex with her, I'd be very curious to know how you do this. I'd be even more curious to know why you'd want to.

Logistics

No matter how good you are at avoiding state breaks, bad logistics can kill your chances:

- Use your house instead of hers for the first time you have sex with someone. A woman's bedroom is full of state breaks waiting to happen. Roommates or family could be at home and break her mood. Her pet could be sick. She could have left her bedroom in a mess and be too embarrassed to show it to you. Neighbors could drop by. In addition, she's reminded more of her daily routine – how much sleep she needs, what she needs to do the next day, etc. You sometimes lose the romantic or party atmosphere at a woman's house.

- Make sure our house is set up for seduction. At a bare minimum, it should be clean, especially the bathroom. Not necessarily spotless, but clean enough for a woman to be comfortable. Have fun things to do if you still need to build comfort. Interactive fun is better than cool DVDs. Use fun truth-or-dare-type games, an easy 3D jigsaw puzzle, whatever.

- The living room (or wherever you plan to bring her first) should be laid out so there is no obvious way for you both to sit down except side-by-side together on a couch. If you have chairs, pile stuff on them or get rid of them before she comes over so she can't sit there.

- Some romance and implied sexuality never hurt. Have champagne, strawberries, and whipped cream around. Don't turn into some nightmarish sleazy gigolo with them, but realize you have them and can break them out when needed. Be fun, not seductive.

- Ensure that your house reflects and supports your identity. If you've been communicating that you are creative and imaginative, but your house is undecorated and full of piles of video games, she'll wonder if you're just an act. I don't need to tell you that that's a bad thing for her to be thinking about when she's trying to decide whether to have sex with you.

- Remove elements of your décor that a woman would find particularly offensive. Most women aren't impressed with public displays of pornography or graphic violence.

- Alcohol can build comfort and also let a woman feel less responsible ("I can justify this to myself because I'm drunk and it just happened, even though in reality I only had two drinks"). Have drinks at home that women like. Many women prefer wine to beer, shooters to shots, vodka to rum, and sweet mixers to bitter ones. Learn the basic differences between wines. You don't need to know specific vineyards or brands, but you should know the basic types of wine (beyond red vs. white) and the difference between good and bad wine. Learn how to make drinks women order when they are having fun. Cosmopolitans and Margaritas are good places to start. And you'll never go wrong with champagne (which need not be expensive). IMPORTANT: We're talking about one or two drinks for her to feel comfortable. Don't get a women drunk to have sex with her. Ethics aside, in many jurisdictions a drunk person cannot legally give consent for sex. The techniques in this book will get you success with many women without having to risk this.

- There is literally an almost endless list of things you can do to improve your house to make it ideal for Seduction, but there's no need to overdo it. Do a good job on your living quarters and then leave it alone; the rest of your time is best spent on other things.

Arousal

There is an incredible amount of information – much of it bad – available on how to arouse women. Techniques for arousal are not covered in detail in this book.

An aroused woman is less likely to be affected by state breaks.

In the meantime, here are a few tips to get you going that correct some common mistakes. These won't make you a good lover by themselves, but they will at least help you avoid being bad in bed:

- Most women can orgasm. Not all the time and not always the first time with someone, but you should be fairly confident of your ability to give a woman an orgasm before penetration. Other men can and will. If you currently have a regular sex partner, swallow your pride and ask her to help you.

- A woman's body is more than two breasts and a vagina. Touch her everywhere. Pay attention to the little spots you like, or she likes.

- Slow it down. You're not in a hurry. Take your time moving from one activity to another.

- Tease her a bit. Most women love to be teased in bed.

- Most women love their hair being pulled and neck kissed and lightly bitten. Learn to do these properly.

- Don't forget the power of language. If you are fingering her, for example, this is a great time to be whispering in her ear how sexy she is, how much you want her, etc. Some women will be into different sorts of verbal stimulation – find out what she likes.

Reassurance

Women will often object to increasing sexual contact. Sometimes they want you to stop. Sometimes they want you to slow down. Sometimes they want you to ignore their objections. Sometimes they want to increase the sexual tension. Sometimes they don't know what they want but their instinctive reaction, for reasons we've already explored in this chapter, is to say no.

Guess what? It doesn't really matter what she wants.

"Stop" means stop. "No" means no. You can try again later or you can try something else, but you can't barrel through. You can't know for sure what's in her head. Even if you could, you can't know what she's going to do the next day. Maybe she has fantasies of being overpowered – not that rare, really – and enjoys having sex despite objecting verbally. Then she kisses you goodbye, goes home, and feels badly about herself and wishes she hadn't had sex. She tells her roommate. It comes out that she did tell you no and you ignored it. Her roommate makes her feel better by telling her that if she tried to say no, what happened wasn't really her fault. The word "rape" comes up. The police get involved. Welcome to hell.

The skillset you will have from mastering the material in this book will lead you to have many options, so it's okay if not all of them pan out, or if you have to see her again before she's ready.

OK, now that we've got that out of the way, let's look at how to handle objections, token or otherwise, in a way that makes her feel comfortable and is safe.

Token objections

The first consideration is verbal. "No," "stop," and "I don't want to do this" are pretty unambiguous. Women who want to make token objections will often say things like "we shouldn't be doing this." A good response to this is to agree with her. Respond with "Yes we shouldn't be doing this... and we definitely shouldn't be doing THIS... you are so bad." Now you've changed the frame from her resisting you to the two of you sharing a conspiracy over doing something you shouldn't be doing, or possibly her trying to seduce you. If she says it again, about the same activity ("No, really, we shouldn't be doing this"), that's a no and you have to stop.

Another example of a token objection comes if you take her home and she says "I'm not going to have sex with you." Don't engage this. You're not going to argue her into committing to having sex with you before you get home. There's especially no reason to argue with her, as sex isn't an imminent option at that point. By the time you and she are on your bed, she might have changed her mind. So either ignore the comment or tease her for being presumptuous. If you argue with her, you risk letting her get locked into a mental position that she's not going to have sex that night: a position she may feel bound to be consistent with later. There's a more advanced tactic of playfully pretending to misinterpret what she is saying as arguing over what kind of you sex you will be having, but this should be reserved for when your skills are very advanced.

If she says "no" and you sense that she doesn't mean it, tell her that, to you, no has to mean no. Don't make it a lecture, just a quick statement and then move back to what you were doing before she said no. Even if you know for sure that she doesn't mean "no," reread the paragraph above that ended with "welcome to hell." If she's really insistent on having you ignore her when she says no, she'll know what a safeword is and how to use it. If you don't know what a safeword is, you're not ready for this kind of situation.

Persistence

She may want you to be persistent, for the same reason that she gave you token objections: she doesn't want to feel easy or for you to think she's easy. When you reach something that she objects to (say, taking off her shirt), go back a step to something she is comfortable with (like touching her breasts with her shirt on) and try again in a few minutes.

Levels of intimacy

It's not only up to the woman to set limits on how far the two of you will go. Traditionally, the man wants sex and will take it if the woman gives it to him, but if she sets a lower limit (like no touching below the waist) he'll take as much as he can get up to that limit. This essentially means that a woman sets the level of intimacy, and that level will be at the upper limit of her comfort zone.

However, it doesn't have to work this way. You can't insist on sex if she isn't willing, but you don't have to accept her chosen substitute. She may want to lie in bed with you and kiss all night. You may want sex. Neither of you is obligated to give the other what they want. Explain to her, without any resentment, that lying in bed with her all night kissing will make you aroused and frustrated and you'd prefer to wait until she's more comfortable with you. Come across as confident and understanding. You have experience with women and you're not going to rush her into something she doesn't want. On the other hand, you're not desperate for sex. The key here is to show absolutely no resentment or annoyance. She will be looking for it. Don't tell her it's all or nothing because she may feel manipulated.
Don't press her to agree to anything verbally, but see what happens when you start sexual touching again. She may let you past her previous resistance point. If she objects again you may need to take a break.

Breaks

Here we use the word "break" to mean pauses during an activity, not to mean state breaks. When you reach a point that she doesn't want to cross, and persistence didn't work, then stop. Say "I understand" with not even the slightest hint of disappointment or annoyance and remove the romantic/sexual frame. Candles, incense, dim lights, mood music – all gone. You're not punishing her, you're just doing something else. After all, you like her and you enjoy her company. Let her know this. Then do something else – ideally something boring. Check your email. Play "go fish" with a deck of cards. She will likely re-initiate physical/sexual contact (if she doesn't, do it yourself in a few minutes). When she does, re-establish the mood with what candles, incense, lights, music, or whatever you were using to begin with. Then proceed slowly to the resistance point, taking your time. If you hit it, or any other resistance point, say "I understand" and repeat the process – wait longer this time if it's you who re-initiates the physical/sexual contact.

Chapter 11: Direct Game

Direct Game

Even though I wrote every word of this book myself, Love Systems is not just about me. We have a team of the top 10-20 dating coaches around the globe who are among the world's most knowledgeable and successful men in terms of succeeding with women and teaching those skills to others.

For this chapter, I wanted to introduce readers to one of our London-based instructors who goes by the name of Soul. If you met him, you'd never think he was a Love Systems instructor. He's short, not especially good looking, and his ethnicity (South Asian) is not necessarily an advantage when dealing with many women. But, he's one of the world's best dating gurus and instructors, and is living proof that the Love Systems approach can work – and produce amazing results – for everyone. It is a privilege to present his thoughts on "Direct Game," one of the most powerful tools in our arsenal. Direct game involves making your intentions known in the initial approach, which conveys a very strong masculine identity. This, in turn, is extremely attractive to women. Over to Soul:

One of the threads running through the chapters on the Emotional Progression Model is that you can vary how "direct" you want to be with a woman. Directness refers to making your romantic/sexual intentions explicit as opposed to implied. The difference between approaches is most noticeable in the early phases (Approaching through Attraction) of the Model.

There are a couple of common misconceptions about direct game that I want to clear up before we go any further. First, direct vs. indirect is a continuum, not an either/or. A strategy can be extremely direct, somewhat direct, slightly indirect, and so on. The range of openers ranked along the risk/ reward scale in Chapter 5 (Approaching) illustrate this.

Second, "explicit" does not mean "sexually graphic". It just means being open about your romantic and/or sexual interest in her. Similarly, "implied" does not mean "unknown". Your interest in each other should be mutually understood at the latest when you're in the Qualification phase anyway.

As explained in Chapter on Approaching, "direct" strategies tend to be higher-risk and higher-reward than more "indirect" tactics. If you go up to ten women and say, "You're gorgeous," you're likely to get into fewer conversations than you would if you used an Indirect Opener. However, those women that do respond well to your opener are much more likely to go on dates with you.

When I first experimented with Direct Game, it was exhilarating, but the challenge was making it work consistently. Years later, I have discovered the underlying foundations of successful Direct Game, to the point where it leads to sexual relationships regularly and frequently. It's a large subject, and one that Love Systems treats in detail in special one-day seminars as well as in other products, but Savoy asked me to contribute some of my experience as a bonus for Magic Bullets, so here goes.

First, let me say that there is no single magic strategy that works on every woman. Learning different skill sets and experimenting with different styles is what ultimately improves your overall ability to build relationships with women. Direct and Indirect are two great examples of this: they are opposite ends of a spectrum and yet both can be spectacularly powerful. I recommend you experiment with both extremes as well as different points along the continuum to see which work best for you. In the long-term, you will maximize your potential by being able to adapt your technique for the specific situation at hand.

As for direct game specifically, start with these 10 steps to direct game success:

1. Build up your pre-approach value. Direct game forces a woman to make a snap decision on whether she is attracted to you enough to have a conversation with you, therefore you need to start from the highest baseline of value as you can. This means looking your absolute best (Chapter 20 on fashion), having strong non-verbal communication (Chapter 17), and flipping as many of the attraction switches from Chapter 7 (Attraction) as you can before you approach her. For example, if you talk to lots of people in the venue and appear to have social value before approaching her, she will have a greater chance of being attracted to you when you do approach because of your Status. (Remember, Status is one of the eight attraction switches, and applies even in a very narrow context like a bookstore or bar).

2. Demonstrating genuine passion and energy is even more important the more direct your strategy. The worst way to tell a woman you like her is without enthusiasm. The more emotion that appears behind what you are saying, the more likely she is to respond positively.

3. For openers, calibrate to the situation. For example, in a bar or club, you can say things like, "You looking fucking sexy in that dress," but in Day Game (Chapter 13) you should be more charming and gentlemanly, "I just saw you walking down the street and thought you looked absolutely beautiful, I had to come say hello."

4. After you approach, do not stand around and wait for a reaction. A Direct opener is not going to make a woman fall at your feet; it's still just a entry point

to a conversation and grounds why you are talking to her. Ask a simple, low investment question, ideally something humorous, and then use a Transition (usually a Content Transition, see Chapter 6 on Transitioning for an review of transitions) such as "what are you up to today?" or, "you're here to pick up guys, aren't you?"

5.   Of the eight attraction switches, Confidence and Humor are among the most useful for building attraction if you are "going direct". Be completely unapologetic and unashamed of your attraction to her – it is very important to be congruent with the attitude of a confident, successful man approaching a beautiful woman. By being direct, you are demonstrating your willingness to take risks for the things you want. Get her laughing as soon as you can. A simple way to do this is to joke about the fact that you are trying to pick her up, e.g. "I thought I should come chat you up before everyone starts getting drunk and you've got a hundred guys grabbing at you. I'm sober now, so you're getting prime conversation here." Qualify her simultaneously as you build Attraction. You've already let her know that you find her attractive, but you need to make her feel good for things specific to her. As you get more signs of attraction (from her to you), give more specific and elaborate compliments. For example, "You have a nice smile" is a generic compliment, whereas, "You have such a nice smile. It's the kind of smile that makes people feel completely relaxed when they are talking to you. I like that," is a very strong compliment. This is somewhat of an exception to the idea that you don't compliment a woman early in your interaction based on her physical features.

6.   Exude sexuality. This is a huge part of being direct. Make small sexual comments early on. For example, in a nightclub, you might say something like "your ass looks incredible in that dress" anytime from the Attraction phase onward. You would then gradually build up the level of sexual energy as the interaction continues. As you get more Attraction and move towards Comfort, sexually project what you want to do with her, e.g. "I'm going to get you wearing those black high heels, a pair of long black gloves, and nothing else." Expressing sexuality is all about calibration and takes practice; be willing to take it too far to find out where the line is.

7.   Being direct doesn't mean dropping the important tactics and boundaries of the Emotional Progression Model. For example, it's just as important – if not more so – to be emotionally open in Comfort, and make a genuine effort to get to know her. When you are talking with her, even in a busy bar, act like you and her are in a tiny bubble of energy and emotion, and the chaotic world outside doesn't even exist.

8.   Use her sexuality to get her aroused, even when you're in public. When you kiss her on the lips, progress to kissing her neck and rubbing her thighs. Whis-

per in her ears the things you want to do her and how aroused she is making you. When she is turned on, stop and continue talking. This will build an incredible amount of sexual tension and it will be easy to lead her to another venue or back to your place.

9.   Move into the Seduction phase as quickly as you can. Being direct means progressing things with a woman as fast as possible, and then adding in more Comfort on an ad hoc basis. Whenever you are worried whether you should try to escalate things or not, escalate. You'll be amazed at what you can recover from. If she rejects an advance, don't pout or sulk, just continue from where you were and try again later.

More Information

Love Systems offers other direct game products including an in-depth audio interview (starring Soul), as well as a one-day specialty seminar on the subject; go to www.LoveSystems.com/Direct for more information or email our program manager at programs@lovesystems.com.

Chapter 12: Social Circle

12

What is your social circle?

Your social circle is your extended network. It includes your friends and acquaint-ances, family, and professional contacts. But it's also bigger than this – a friend of a friend is in your extended social circle. If you are a very social person, your social circle can include people several degrees of separation from you. As a general rule, someone is in your social circle if you can be introduced to him or her by someone else in your circle who knows both of you reasonably well.

In general, it is far easier to be with a woman in your social circle than it is with a stranger. However, the risks involved make social circle gaming something I would recommend only for men who have developed the skills that come from mastering the material in this book. Your social circle is not a place to practice. Get your prac-tice time in at bars, clubs, concerts, coffee shops, restaurants, bookstores, thea-tres, parks, beaches, on public transportation, or anywhere else you can meet people. Your social circle will still be there when you're ready.

By the way, this chapter is only focused on how developing relationships within your social circle is different from developing relationships via cold approach. Build-ing and expanding your social circle is another subject entirely, and the subject of an upcoming Love Systems product[7].

Social circle – advantages

Learn the built-in benefits of social circle gaming so you can take advantage of them.

- Your value is assumed to be higher than if you met her at a bar, and is of-ten reasonably assumed to be reasonably close to hers.

  People tend to interact with others of similar social status. They also tend to make preliminary judgments about others based in part on the context in which they meet. If I told you I was going to introduce you to Jessica Alba's best friend, you would likely as-sume that you are about to meet an attractive woman. If a woman values and respects her friends, she will likely assume

---

[7] Check out www.LoveSystems.com or e-mail us at info@lovesystems.com for information and updates.

their friends to be high-value as well. Of course this is just your starting point and will not save you if you display low-value behavior.

- She is more likely to learn about, and believe, good things that you have going for you.

  If you make a good impression on a woman she might ask other people in her social circle about you. If they tell her how great you are and how wonderful you'd be for each other, her interest in you will be solidified. This is the same thing as Personal Source DHVs from Chapter 7. Review this chapter if you plan to do much social circle gaming.

- She should be less "flaky."

  There are a lot of factors that might make women cancel on or not show up for dates (covered in Chapter 9: Comfort and Chapter 22: Phone Game). Many of these are less relevant if you are connected to her social circle. Similarly, women tend to avoid awkwardness or loss of face in their social circle. Canceling at the last minute on a date with someone she met at a coffee shop doesn't carry any social consequences. Canceling on someone she might see again can be awkward.

- She should trust you more easily.

  Women often won't want to be alone with a man they don't know, particularly in vulnerable situations (e.g., late at night, at his house, in sexual situations, etc.). A woman will more readily trust a man who is known within her circle and can be vouched for.
  For example, as a stranger, she might not let you give her a ride home from an event. As a friend-of-a-friend, she might, which then allows you to talk in private, build a connection, and possibly give you an opportunity that you might otherwise not have had.

- You can interact with her without her thinking that you are hitting on her.

  If you've been introduced to someone connected to your social circle, it will usually be natural to get to know her. She won't likely wonder "why is he talking to me?" as much as if a stranger had approached her at a bar. You likely won't have to disqualify yourself or break through her barriers right away. (See Chapter 7 for more on disqualification and barriers.)

- You don't have to Approach or Transition.

  If you are introduced to someone, it is assumed that you are in a normal conversation with them. This puts you in the Attraction phase (Chapter 7).

- You have more time to make a positive impression.

  If it is "normal" to talk to her as part of your social circle, you won't be as much "on the clock" or immediately judged by your first impression. If you are part of a large group doing something social together (drinks after work, a concert, a party), a woman will give you more time to win her attention. She won't want the group to think that she is rude to someone in their circle.

  Unlike if you were a stranger, her friends will be less likely to interrupt your interaction with her to "protect" her.

  Logistics become much easier. As a stranger, when her group moves from one venue to another, it can be difficult and require some skill to encourage her to stay with you, to join her group, or to get a solid phone number. As part of her circle, you can naturally move with the group.

  If you see a woman regularly (e.g., at work or at regular social occasions), you don't have to get to the Comfort phase in the first interaction, like you would have to with a stranger. You know you'll see her again.

- She can observe your good qualities rather than your having to tell her about them.

  Recall in Chapter 7 on Attraction that a woman will give more weight to what she can perceive about you directly than what you tell her about yourself. This has special relevance to your social circle if you are going to see a woman repeatedly. For example, if you see the same group of friends every Friday for happy hour and one Friday you bring an attractive woman, the other women there may think that you are Pre-selected (Chapter 3). At next week's happy hour when you arrive alone, they may be more curious about you.

- Building comfort is vastly easier.

    You already have overlapping social circles, so you have plenty of opportunity to talk about mutual friends and contacts. You've probably had shared experiences and have some shared interests. This is a great starting point from which to build comfort.

Social Circle – Disadvantages

The disadvantages of social circle gaming are relatively small and are usually straightforward to deal with. Still, it's best to be aware of them so you can avoid obvious pitfalls:

- Women do not want to feel "easy" or be made a fool of in front of their social circle.

    A woman may be less likely to have sex with you early on in your interaction with her if you are in her social circle. She'll be worried about her friends finding out and thinking she is easy, or of seeing you again and feeling awkward. Keep any sexual touching or conversation away from her friends and convey to her, through your actions and through storytelling, that you are discreet and have good Social Intuition.

- Some women say they do not "go out with people from work" or "date their friends."

    This one is a bit of a red herring. Sure, you might find a rare woman who adheres strictly to this rule in all situations, but most women will toss it aside if they meet someone sufficiently captivating. Usually it's just an excuse – like when a woman tells you out of the blue that she has a boyfriend. This can happen when you have communicated too much interest in her too early (or, in terms of the Emotional Progression Model, you are trying to build comfort before you have created sufficient Attraction).

- You need to be "on" for a lot more time.

If you meet her as a stranger, you only have to be at your best long enough for a sexual relationship to develop. If you see a woman every day at work, you have to be "on" for most of that time. This doesn't mean that you should go into work with the same high-energy entertaining persona that you use at night-clubs. It does mean that you have much more chance to lose value through having a bad day or just doing something socially awkward or unattractive.

Social Circle – Strategies

Succeeding with a woman in your social circle is a variation on what you'd do if she were a stranger, not a completely new system. Here are some additional tips to keep in mind:

- Slow it down and tone it down. Social circle gaming should happen at a quarter to half of your "cold approach" speed and energy level.

- Peer endorsement is crucial. It's important enough if you're approaching her as a stranger, since her friends should like you enough to encourage her to leave with you or to see you again.

- It's extra important when dealing with mutual friends since they know you and she'll trust their judgment. Cultivate your friends. Time spent managing your social circle is rarely time wasted.

- Be very careful with Attraction material. What can seem playful or normal in a high-energy social environment (disqualifiers, negs, etc.) can be very inappropriate in a social circle setting.

- Until mutual interest is solidly established, dates are often unnecessary. She's in your circle, so invite her and everyone else out for something fun, like drinks after work, dinner, or a trip to a club. On the surface, you're just being social (and demonstrating that you have Status within the group, since you're the one organizing and making plans). If she's interested in you, she'll make sure she's there.

- Do not put a woman in a potentially embarrassing position. Don't kiss her where anyone else can see. Don't get into a lot of touching that would draw attention to her and you. Once there is mutual interest and sexual tension, then some discreet "under the table" or "behind the back" touching can be alright, since it adds an element of the forbidden and scandalous.

- Getting into the Seduction phase can be difficult when mutual friends or coworkers are around. She generally won't want anyone to know what is happening. However, she likely won't help you get around this problem, because she doesn't want to have to participate in her own seduction. This is your job. In this situation, you can try to meet up with her another time for a date, but then you lose the emotional momentum from the current interaction and she has all the intervening time to think about whether she really wants to be sexual with you or with someone in her social circle generally. Or, use one of the techniques below to get her alone with you at the right time, without anyone noticing or her feeling awkward:

    Offer her a ride home if she came without a car, or offer to walk her home.

    Ask her for a ride home. Even better, get one of your friends to say he needs to leave early and have him ask her to drive you home later since you'd otherwise be stranded. This is a great wingman strategy; see Chapter 21 on Winging for more of those.

    Just wait. Other people will leave and you might get lucky and end up as the last two people there. If this happens, it's almost certain that she is interested in you.

    Change venues frequently to "shake people off." If you all went to a restaurant, and people start leaving after dinner, you can invite whoever is left to go with you to a bar down the street where you are supposedly meeting friends. It won't be as awkward for her to come along, but you have a decent chance of getting rid of some people in your group by doing so.

Social Circle – Risks

I strongly believe that the advantages of meeting women through your social circle far outweigh the disadvantages. However, I don't recommend that you use the techniques from Magic Bullets or other Love Systems training material in your social circle until you are extremely comfortable with them. This is because of the risks involved:

- While the techniques in this book are powerful, they require some practice. It is easy to make social errors and create awkwardness when starting out. I certainly did. Fortunately, if you inadvertently offend a stranger you meet in a coffee shop, she might tell her friends, but it won't affect your life. If you make someone in your social circle uncomfortable, word will get around. Other women in your circle will be warned about you, and you jeopardize your standing in your social circle generally. Don't do this. The value of your social circle goes far beyond it being a potential source of women to date.

- Even if you don't commit any social errors, getting rejected within your social circle more than once or twice can hurt your chances in the future. In technical terms, women will Observe your lack of Pre-selection. In straight English, women don't like to date their friends' rejects. You also may lose status within the group every time you are rejected.

- Any time your social circle includes professional contacts, the risks are multiplied.

- Even if you are successful with women in your social circle, you risk developing a reputation – this time as a "player." While some women find it exciting to meet and be seduced by a man who is obviously experienced with women, few women want to be "Conquest #14" in their social circle. Especially when they would have to see Conquests 1-13 and the player in question whenever they hang out with their friends. In some social circles it's "okay" for people to hook up casually, but this isn't the case most of the time.

Workplace romance Examples

A workplace romance is a particularly tricky element of social circle game. The workplace is definitely not the place to practice. To mix things up a bit, I will use the His Version / Her Version style that I use in the Love Systems' insider (LSi), the free Love Systems online training course (sign up at: www.LoveSystems.com/insider).

When reading these stories, try to figure out what the man did wrong or right in each example before reading ahead.

Example 1: John's version

I'm a finance manager at XYZ Corp. One day, I noticed an attractive woman in marketing. For the next little while I saw her in the halls or the elevator, and we'd say hi and smile. A couple of weeks later I got up the courage to go to her desk and talk to her. We chatted for a while and then I asked her out for drinks after work, but she already had plans. We kept seeing each other around, and every once in a while I'd go over to chat and ask her out but she always seemed to have things to do. I just have to wait until she gets less busy and then I'll take my shot.

Example 1: Emily's version

I just started in marketing at XYZ Corp. My co-workers are great, but there's this creepy guy in Finance who hits on me all the time. I thought he was cute when I first saw him, but he never talked to me until all of a sudden he starts coming over and hanging out when I'm working. It was really obvious. He asked me out in front of everyone and it became a joke among all of us. Jessica the receptionist said he does the same thing to her.

Well, that didn't work very well, did it? Let's let John try again.

Example 2: John's version

I'm a finance manager at XYZ Corp. One day, I noticed an attractive woman in marketing. She was new, so I said hi, and I, and introduced her around to other people in the company. We saw each other around and would sometimes stop and chat. If I had to go to marketing for something and it was a slow day, I'd sometimes stop for a bit to talk with her and Melanie and Don, who sit by her. Every few weeks, a bunch of us go to bar for dinner and karaoke after work, so tonight I invited the three of them along.

Example 2: Emily's version

I just started in marketing at XYZ Corp. My co-workers are great, and there's a really cute guy in Finance who I like. He was one of my first friends when I started, and we chat or joke around sometimes. He always makes me laugh, and Don and Melanie have good things to say about him. Anyway, he told us that some of the folks were going for dinner and karaoke tonight so of course I'll be there.

Now, let's take a look at how to take the relationship further. This gets a bit harder.

Example 3: John's version

> We were out at dinner, and I sat next to Emily. Over a few drinks, we talked a lot. I really felt myself getting somewhere. I got some touching going too, like I had my arm around her after dessert for a few minutes. I made a move on her on the dance floor later on, but she said she doesn't date people from work.

Example 3: Emily's version

> We were out at dinner, and John sat next to me. He got really drunk and kept trying to get me to drink. He was really obvious and kept monopolizing my attention so I could only talk to him. When he put his arm around me, I didn't do anything about it because I didn't want to be rude, but I was giving "save me" glances to my friends. He tried to kiss me on the dance floor so I had to give him some excuse to get rid of him. Ugh.

Okay, that one was exaggerated for effect. Let's try something a bit better. Keep trying to guess where things are going right and wrong when reading John's story.

Example 4: John's version

> We were out at dinner, and I sat next to Emily. I made sure to talk with everyone, telling great stories, with everyone listening. A couple of times, Emily and I had little side conversations, with lots of flirting and casual but friendly touching. After dinner, I caught her alone coming out of the bathroom where no one could see and kissed her. It was a long, passionate makeout, and a giant release of sexual tension. We were hot for each other. I told her we'd need to continue this later with no one around and she agreed. An hour later I told her to say she had car trouble so I'd need to give her a ride home, but she was busy talking to her friends. I sat with her to try to get her attention back to our plan. When she came out of the bathroom later, I tried to do the same kiss move again, but this time it felt awkward and she said our friends would be looking for us. I explained that they didn't catch us the first time, so they wouldn't catch us this time, but she was already moving back. A few minutes later I saw her dancing with some guy on the dance floor

floor and giving him her phone number. I went in to make my move before it got too far, told her I was leaving and offered her a ride home (hint, hint). She said she needed to stay with her friends, so I left alone. Today, she told me she was drunk last night and the kiss shouldn't have happened.

Example 4: Emily's version

We were out at dinner, and John sat next to me. I was still really attracted to him at first, and then we shared a really hot kiss by the bar. That sort of got it out of the system for me, but he wanted more. He was all clingy and creepy, and tried to hang off of me the rest of the night – totally not the guy I thought he was! I had an awkward moment this morning letting him down.

Let's break this one down and see what really happened...

John did everything right until the kiss. The kiss was unnecessary there and then. John probably did it to make sure that Emily was into him. That might have been okay if it were quick, but a long drawn-out makeout actually dissipated the sexual tension. John was no longer someone Emily was trying to attract; she knew she had him already. He should have let the sexual tension continue to build until he was in a place where he could have taken advantage of it. Chapter 18 (Kissing) explains this psychological process in more detail.

After the kiss, things really went downhill. John became submissive and clingy instead of the confident man Emily had been attracted to. He tried to involve Emily in a little conspiracy to be alone together, which bored her and turned her off. As an attractive woman, she knows how to get alone with men. She's also been alone with men who made everything feel natural. This didn't feel very natural or fun to her. Then John started retracing old ground (the same kiss) hoping to re-create the earlier result. This sealed his fate. For John to have won her back that night, he probably would have needed to introduce an element of jealousy by casually flirting with someone else, preferably someone from outside the group.

Let's give John one last chance.

Example 5: John's version

We were out at dinner, and I sat next to Emily. I had a great time, talking with everyone, telling great stories, with everyone listening. A couple of times, Emily and I had little side conversations, with lots of flirting and casual but friendly touching. I was hanging out with other people after dinner, but we kept gravitating back to each other. When there were only 5 of us left, I suggested we all go to a club down the street where my friend was DJing and I was meeting some friends. Emily said she'd come along, so I made a big show of trying to convince the others to come too so it didn't look obvious, and to give Emily more of a challenge. Samuel from accounting did come along, but I kept feeding him alcohol and introducing him to women until he disappeared. Emily and I had a quick kiss on the dance floor, which I stopped first. An hour later, we left together.

Example 5: Emily's version

We were out at dinner, and John sat next to me. I was pretty into him, so when he was about to go to this club down the street, I went with him. I told Melanie that I'd just take a taxi home, but I wanted to stay out a bit longer and party. Samuel from accounting followed me, of course, since he's always hitting on me, but John did a great job getting rid of him without making it awkward. I ended up back at John's apartment an hour later. I told him I could only come in for a minute, but now it's 7 a.m. and I have to go home and change!

Now that's how it's done. You can read plenty of "field reports" like these at The Attraction Forums (www.TheAttractionForums.com). It's free!

To learn more about Social Circles and how to get the most out of yours, the Love Systems Social Circle Mastery program (www.LoveSystems.com/Social-Circle) is the best in the business.

Chapter 13: Day Game

13

Day Game

For a discussion of Day Game, I decided to bring back an expert. Soul is not just the Love Systems go-to guy for direct game, he's also the master of meeting a woman anywhere outside of "traditional" night-time social venues like bars, clubs, restaurants, etc. Day Game includes, but is not limited to, meeting women on the street, in cafes, parks, shopping malls, gyms, art galleries, and college campuses. Over to Soul:

When I started learning Day Game, I thought it was impossible and ridiculous to approach a woman who I didn't know in the middle of the day. I imagined that no one really did it and that I'd be rejected immediately. I've since learned that to pick up a woman during the day is possible – common, actually – and fun. Day Game is now a staple of mine and I have met many of my favourite women, including my long term relationships, through Day Game.

First, let's take a look at what makes Day Game different.

Advantages

1. Mastering Day Game as well as Night Game means you can meet women, anywhere, anytime. Because you don't specifically have to go out to do Day Game (though it helps to do so), you can fit approaches into your everyday schedule, thus maximizing your time and opportunity for meeting women.

2. You meet a greater variety (and some would say quality) of beautiful women. Some women simply don't like going out to "traditional" night-time venues or don't go very often. Others may not have the time. For example, an educated, professional woman in a real job probably isn't at the local hot spot at 2am on a Tuesday morning because she has to work the next day. But she will be on the street, at a coffee shop, at a mall, or any number of other places where you could meet her the next day.

3. Women are approached far less often during the day than they are in clubs and bars at night. This means that you will be more memorable. She'll (hopefully) be sober too, which will also help for this. So instead of being one of five men she met during a blurry, slightly-drunk night in a dark club, you'll be that interesting man who charmed her at her local coffee shop. This will help a ton in your subsequent Phone Game (Chapter 22) and in setting up a future Date (Chapter 16).

4. There's a Day Game venue for everyone. Don't like nightclubs? Have a night job or early-morning responsibilities? No problem. Spend Saturday afternoon in a busy park meeting women and see how much more fun you have. suits some men really well, for example older men that don't feel comfortable in loud nightclubs, or men that don't have as much time to go out every weekend.

5. Practicing Day Game emphasizes different areas of the Emotional Progression Model (e.g. the Comfort phase) and therefore helps to develop areas that you may be less focussed upon in Night Game.

6. You will rarely see beautiful women alone in bars and clubs. As you've seen in Chapters 5-8, a lot of what you're doing in the early stages of your interaction in Night Game has to do with navigating through her friends and attracting her when she's in a larger group. You are much more likely to find a beautiful woman by herself in Day Game, which makes the process a lot easier. However, this isn't a reason to avoid groups during the day...this can still work just as well.

Disadvantages

1. People often aren't in a socializing frame of mind when they are going about their day. They are sometimes slightly surprised or defensive when they are approached. Most of the strangers who have approached you in the past probably wanted something – spare change, cigarettes, etc. – and the same is probably true for her too. This may influence her initial reaction to your approach, but this isn't all bad news; her surprise may stimulate stronger emotions in the women you approach, which gives you more to work with.

2. Daytime situations tend to be subject to higher social pressure. More people can hear and see what you're saying and doing. This means you need to be willing to let other people overhear your pick ups in coffee shops, subway carriages, bookstores etc. This is mostly relevant only to the early stages of the Emotional Progression Model, as other people get bored quickly and generally stop listening. However, it does mean that she might be a little more self-conscious.

3. Women can often have legitimate time constraints during the day. At a bar, it's assumed that there's nowhere else that she has to be, but during the day she may be running errands or on her way somewhere. To use an extreme example, Savoy likes to meet women in the elevator in his office building – which

probably has something to do with there being a casting agency on the top floor. In such situations, you may have to work much more quickly than you are used to, and getting a solid phone number is more important.

Venues and Strategies

One of the beautiful aspects of Day Game is the sheer variety of venues where you can meet women and what you can do with them. Let's take some common examples:

- **The Street:** This is my favorite venue because you get constant streams of beautiful women walking past, provided you pick the right street of course. Shopping streets are ideal, but beware of times when they're overcrowded. In such cases, go to quieter streets, or simply find less crowded areas of the street, e.g. nearer the kerb or near the store windows. Also, be aware that people are constantly going in and out of stores, crossing roads etc., so when you see a woman you want to approach you generally need to do so quickly lest she changes trajectory suddenly and it starts to look like you're stalking her. You can some get away with a little hesitation in bars and clubs (though it's not ideal and you should try to eliminate it) because the women aren't going anywhere, but on the street you need to act quickly. Also, don't think that a woman walking is harder to approach than a woman standing still; you just need to be confident enough in your opener and have strong enough body language to stop her. Direct Openers (Chapter 5) work extremely well on the street and have a romantic element to them that women love (it's a better story to tell her friends that a guy picked her up while she was out shopping than picked her up in a bar). Opinion Openers or low key Indirect Openers, e.g. "Do you know where the nearest decent coffee shop is?", also work well but make sure you have a solid Transition (Chapter 6) ready to go.

- **Shopping Malls:** These are always full of good-looking women, either hanging out by themselves, or more commonly in groups. Opinion Openers work great in these situation as you can really ground them to your environment. For example, you can approach some women and say: "guys, I need to a present for my cousin; where do you think I can get the cutest kids' clothes from around here?" If she's with friends, best strategy is often to make friends with the whole group, and then invite them all out to a venue that you're going to that night (the further in the future the event is, the more attraction and comfort you'll have to build to prevent her from "flaking"). A good line to use is, "whose number should I take?", as you'll either be given the number of the woman who is most interested in you, or simply the woman who is the most efficient contact to have to leverage the group's decisions. How they react to this question will give you some useful information.

- **Stores:** There's a huge variety of stores that you can have a lot of fun with. Bookstores and music stores are great because you can meet women that have similar tastes to you and come up with some really simple but effective Openers grounded to the section you're in, e.g. "Who do you think is hotter, Snoop Dogg or Akon?" The Openers don't need to be particular elaborate, but make sure you have some good Transition material. Content Transitions work amazingly well here, e.g. if you're in a travelling section of a bookstore you can work in some stories about places you've visited. You can also run Cold Reads based on her tastes. The caveat I'd add to approaching women in stores is to be very aware of your surroundings. First, certain stores are less conducive to approaching (e.g. you'd have to work hard to establish credibility for why you're in a women's lingerie store); second, don't do too many approaches in a small area in rapid succession – women (or even store security) will notice, and you'll face a lot of resistance when you approach.

- **Coffee Shops:** You won't always find huge volumes of beautiful women here in the same way you might a bar a club, but you will spot the occasional woman or group or women you want to approach. Coffee shops have a unique characteristic that people are usually sitting down and static instead of being on the move. At coffee shops, it can often be best to start with a Functional Opener, or even an Opinion Opener with a clear Time Constraint, and then position yourself near her, i.e. sit at a table near her. From there, relax and don't appear too eager to get into a conversation. It helps if you've got a book or laptop so you have a reason why you're there. A minute or so later, re-open the conversation with a second, more involved opener, or a Transition. With this sort of strategy, you gradually build up her investment in the interaction without putting her under pressure to do so. A great coffee shop tactic is to ask her to watch your laptop while you go to the restroom, and then come back and continue a conversation as if its the most natural thing in the world.

- **Museums/Art Galleries:** These venues don't necessarily have a high flow of beautiful women passing through, but suit men who are looking for older, more creative-minded women. Approach here similarly to how you would in stores, but ground your Openers to the specific environment around you. Capitalize on the slightly enhanced level of emotion (creative venues tend to stimulate women emotionally) by cold reading extensively and moving quickly into Comfort (don't go running loud Attraction routines in a quiet gallery).

- **Buses, Trains and Subways:** Depending on what city you live in, public transport game can be an amazing way to maximize your time and opportunity for women. Be strategic. In some cities (e.g., London, New York, Toronto, San Francisco) it is normal for beautiful women to be on the subway or a bus. In others (e.g., Los Angeles, Philadelphia, San Diego) a little less so. Even in "good" cities, it will take you a few approaches to get used to the increased social pressure of Approaching in a quiet subway car, but once you do you realise it's similar to any other Day Game venue. As with coffee shops, many men find it easier open indirectly to avoid putting her under pressure. Newspapers, magazines, books etc. all provide good fodder for grounding your openers. Realise you'll probably have only a few minutes before her stop, so you need to make a good impression quickly and build as much Comfort as you can to make the phone number solid.

Newbie Missions

Doing Day Game can be scary at first. Here are a couple of ideas to ease you into it if you're having trouble. These tasks are progressively harder, but will demonstrate to you that people are a lot friendlier and pleasant in the daytime than you might expect.

- Ask 5 beautiful women what the time is

- Ask 5 beautiful women for directions to the nearest coffee shop

- Ask 5 beautiful women for the nearest men's fashion store, and ask for any men's fashion tips they can think of

- Tell 5 beautiful women that they are cute

Your overarching strategy in Day Game should be to spend as much time with her as possible in the first meeting. You should have a primary goal of taking her on an "instant date" (like going to grab a bite to eat) and a secondary goal of getting a solid phone number. For either of these goals, the more time you can spend with her in Comfort the better, so take her for a coffee or go for a walk with her if you can. However, this won't always be possible if she is busy or in a rush, but at the very least you should walk with her for a few second or move her from where she was to a new location with you. Whatever your chosen venue, have a logistical plan of where you can move her to that's nearby.

Managing logistics like this will improve your success in Day Game quite dramatically.

Finally, here's a bit of troubleshooting for Day Game that reflects a couple of key lessons that I learned the hard way.

1. Don't try to progress physically (Chapter 15) fast as you would in a bar or club. It's fine to touch her a little when you first meet her (e.g. a hand-shake, a light touch on the arm), but you don't want to be throwing your arm around her shoulder or putting your hand on her waist like you might do in a club a few minutes into the interaction. Be sensitive to what she feels comfortable with.

2. Don't focus too much on Attraction. The fact that you've approached her in the day already shows a lot of confidence and you'll find that you can build Attraction more quickly that you would in a bar or club. Focus on Qualifying and building enough Comfort to make sure she remembers you positively.

More Information

The best source of information on Day Game anywhere is the Love Systems Day Game Workshop (www.LoveSystems.com/Day-Game), a full one day workshop that includes both a seminar portion and live in-field training. You can also contact programs@LoveSystems.com if you're interested in specialized live in-person training. If you like what read here, feel free to ask for me personally.

You can also learn a lot more about Day Game by browsing The Attraction Forums. Do a search for "Day Game" articles to see what other men are discussing in the real world.

Chapter 14: Strip Cubs

14

Strip Clubs

Strippers and "stripper game" is outside the scope of this book. However, as a bonus, I am including 10 "strip club rules" by Sinn from the original version of Magic Bullets.

Strip Clubs by Sinn

Many strippers ("exotic dancers") are exceptionally beautiful. Unfortunately, they are also hit on all night long and celebrated for their looks and sexuality. The strip club environment poses some unique challenges. Here are some of my most important tactics and techniques:

1. Time your visits. At the very beginning (1st to 4th) or end (after the 25th) of the month, debts and bills pile up. Many women become strippers because they have money problems. When money pressure becomes more intense, they need to focus more on making money than on getting picked up.

2. Avoid the "customer frame." Many strippers have a rule not to date customers. Once you pay her for anything, you are a customer and a potential recurring source of income. That's more valuable to most strippers than another guy who wants to date her.

3. Avoid "Pervert Row," the first row in front of stage. Remember in Chapter 7 when Savoy explained how a woman's first impression of you comes in part from the context in which she meets you and her experiences with previous men in that context? Put it this way – her experiences with men on Pervert Row won't encourage her to get to know you.

4. Establish a friend on the inside, ideally a man in a power position like the manager or DJ. The best way I have found to do this is to ask who I would talk to about setting up a bachelor party next weekend. Then have the manager walk you around the club explaining everything. Offer to buy him a drink as he does this. If an exotic dancer sees you having a drink with the manager, she will assume you have higher value than the average customer.

5. Control the conversation. Everything that a stripper says to you in the first five minutes is a routine. When they ask what you do or how your night has been, change the topic. Make sure that you stick to your material. You need to select the conversational topics that will make her attracted to you.

6. Sit alone if you want to be approached. To strippers, customers are approaches and she is more comfortable approaching a single man than a group.

7. Stay away from all sexual topics. Make sure she does the same.

8. Stay out of the "here and now." Don't mention the club or the situation you are in. You want her thinking about and feeling things not related to her job as a stripper. You want to convey your personality while displaying both the attributes and characteristics of an attractive man.

9. Make sure she knows you are a "stripper boyfriend" type. Many men can't handle the reality of dating a stripper, and strippers know this. If you communicate or imply that you already have, or that you have an understanding of her world, she will be less nervous about giving you a chance.

10. Related to the above - demonstrate authority over her world. Show her that you are a club insider (not a regular customer), by explaining her life to her. You need to be able to explain to her what her job is really about (approaching men and trying to convince them they have a chance with her). You also need to avoid asking typical questions like "do your parents know?" Make sure that you act bored by her world. I even go so far as to say that I know her world better than she does.

To learn more about the world of exotic dancers and other seemingly unattainable women, and the specialized skill set you need to approach and attract them, Love Systems offers an exclusive Strippers and Hired Guns seminar (www.LoveSystems.com/Strippers).

15

Physical Progression

Chapters 4 to 10 took you through the Emotional Progression phases of the Triad Model to build a romantic and/or sexual relationship with a woman. As the Model teaches, at the same time as you are building emotional intimacy, you must also be building physical intimacy. The Love Systems methodology includes both an emotional and a physical progression model (as well as the third logistical progression model discussed elsewhere). Think of it like two trains running along parallel tracks. One can get ahead of the other, but at the end of the day you need both to reach their destination. (Accordingly, you also need to progress logistically to where you and the woman can be alone somewhere where sex could happen.)

General rules of touching

You don't want to leave touching too late in your interaction. Increasing physical intimacy should be a natural and gradual escalation, not a sudden change of gears accompanied by a big awkward moment when you "make your move."

Touch is also subject to different cultural norms. This chapter is primarily based on experiences in North America, Western Europe, Australia, and South Africa. Latin and East Asian cultures, among others, have different cultural expectations around touch and personal space. Make adjustments accordingly.

Physical progression can be divided into two broad phases, which we discuss later in this chapter:

Social touching, during which you should not really be doing anything differently with the woman you are interested in than with the rest of the group. Even if you are alone with her, the frame for your touching should be social as opposed to romantic or sexual.

Personal touching, in which you use touching to reinforce or lead the emotional connection you are developing with her. Increasing physical intimacy in this way builds comfort and arousal.

Many men who are new to this type of material find that physical progression is a difficult subject at first. This is natural. Like any complicated activity, from learning to drive to playing a sport, there is a lot to keep in mind at the same time and you can only focus on so many elements at once. I tend to encourage men to become comfortable with the Emotional Progression Model first, and then to focus on improving their physical progression skills.

You will need to push through your own discomfort at first and do your best to seem comfortable with each physical step you make. As you get used to it, physicality will get easier and become a natural part of the way you interact with people.

In general, the "go first" principle applies most of the time. Your actions should communicate to her that touching is normal, fun and comfortable by initiating it and being emotionally comfortable with doing it. This will help her follow your lead and be comfortable as well.

Sometimes it's easy to get used to physical progression, or even just to start the process off, by using routines which have a physical component. For example, even a simple routine like saying something funny or apparently insightful about a woman (the latter case usually being a "cold read" – see Chapter 6) based on what rings she is wearing on what fingers gives you an opportunity to touch her. We tend to build progressively-increasing touching into our routines. You can check out a couple hundred scripts that our master instructors use in the Love Systems Routines Manual at www.LoveSystems.com/Routines.

Social Touching

Social touching only includes touching in ways that would be acceptable in a non-romantic context. For example, you can touch someone's arm or shoulder to emphasize a point. You can pat someone on the upper back to congratulate them. Stay away from other areas.

Some general rules:

- **Start early.** It can feel awkward and forced if you start touching someone once you've already been interacting with her for 20 minutes. Start during the opener if you can.

- **Touch everyone in the group**. You want to come across as a social person, not as a creepy seducer. Don't touch the woman you're interested in any differently than you would other strangers. Touch the men too. Studies have shown that people feel better about the people they are talking with if they are occasionally being touched as part of the conversation. Politicians "glad handle" potential voters for a reason.

- **Physical progression should be consistent with emotional progression**. If you are in Qualification, you can use touch to express approval (or to release that approval). In Attraction, your touch should generally be high-energy and interactive, such as challenging a woman to a game of thumb-wrestling.

- **Test her**. Women often give off confusing or mixed signals verbally, but very few "lie" with touching. For example, if you put your arm around a woman, is her first reaction to slide closer to you or to put her arm around your waist? Or does she let your arm just sit there awkwardly? When you take her hand, does she curl her fingers into yours or is her hand limp? Does she pull awkwardly away after a few seconds? When I am not sure of a woman's level of interest in me, I will often do something like this to "check physically."

- **Create opportunities for social touching**. You can make up secret handshakes. You can teach her what the lines on her palm mean (be creative, make her laugh). You can touch her at key moments in your stories. As you gain experience and comfort with particular stories that you tell, you can also anticipate and plan for specific moments when touching fits well with and enhances what you are saying. Or you can develop stories or routines that are specifically designed to allow for social touching. For example, I tell a (true) story about accidentally making out with my roommate's sister in college. Yes, it's possible to accidentally make out with someone. No, it's not something you can teach or plan for. At one point in the story, I mention how I felt a hand on me and say "like this" and put her hand on my forearm. I continue the story without pausing or drawing attention to what I'm doing. While I am telling the rest of the story, I am waiting to see how long it will take her to remove her hand, whether she gives my forearm a little squeeze, etc.

- **Don't let other men touch you without responding**. Men invading other men's personal space is a sign of dominance. Socially dominant men (within the bounds of good social intuition) are generally very attractive to women, and submissive men are not. A recent study showed that women are three to four times more likely to seek to make eye contact with men (i.e. "approach initiations," see Chapter 5) who express this sort of dominance over other men than with men who do not.

Personal Touching

Personal touching is more intimate. Generally it should only take place when you are alone with a woman, or when the rest of her group is obviously comfortable with the increasing intimacy between you and her and she is not embarrassed.

Some examples of personal touching include:

- Her hand on your arm.

- Her hand on your leg.

- Holding hands.

- Your arm around her.

- Her sitting on your lap.

Personal touching is where the "progression" really takes place. You want an over-all increase in your level of physical intimacy with a woman. And it's you who has to guide this process. You decide when to initiate, when to escalate, and when to pull back.

For example, if you are holding hands with her for a while and you get the sense that she is uncomfortable and about to pull away, then you should ideally be the one who breaks the physical contact first. This has the psychological effect of making you the one who is setting the barriers, not her. This will be an unfamiliar but also somewhat comfortable position for many women.

When you break the physical touching, break it completely. Let's take an example in which a woman is comfortable holding hands with you, but not with having your arm around her. If you sense that she is becoming uncomfortable, you should of course be the one to pull back. However, do not only remove your arm and pull back to her comfort point, where you are holding hands. Doing so may make her feel comfortable again, but she will not necessarily feel a desire to increase the intensity of your physical contact. After all, holding hands, in this example, was her desired level of contact at that moment. Cut off the physical contact completely, or at least well below her comfort level. Now she will feel the loss of comfort from holding your hand, may be more responsive when you re-initiate contact.

You should also establish as much of the touching as possible as if she were the initiator. Putting her hand on your arm or your leg is better than putting yours on hers. For one thing, this is far less threatening; she still feels in control with the increased escalation because she can remove herself at any moment; whereas if it is you touching her, she may worry that she may have to "play defense" against your persistent efforts to escalate past her comfort zone. A second reason why this is valuable is because a woman's psychological processes may encourage her to act consistently with her physical behavior. She doesn't generally sit on a man's lap if she doesn't like him.

Doing these things should give her the feeling that she can be as free as she wants to touch you (touching feels good after all) without you putting her in an uncomfortable position. In fact, seducing you can become a fun and interesting challenge for her. Obviously, you will need to go through this a few times before you're able to recognize the feeling of a woman about to pull away.

At the same time, as you are controlling the duration of touching within a given level of physical intimacy, you should be managing the intensity by progressively testing and pushing her boundaries. If she is comfortable holding hands, put her on your lap. If she's comfortable on your lap, bite her neck. Find out where her resistance point is and periodically test to see if you can move past it.

This might feel awkward at first. The average man is not used to the idea of putting a woman on his lap and then pushing her off a few seconds later and playfully telling her to stop trying to seduce him. This doesn't make sense to many men, but it works with women.

Escalating personal touching works best if you aren't drawing attention to what you are doing. Don't ever talk about it. In fact, escalation is easier if there is something going on to distract her as we saw in Chapter 10: Seduction. If one of you is on the telephone, look at this as an opportunity to playfully increase the intensity of your touching. You may have to pull back after the telephone call is over, but by breaking into that territory for a while, you will increase your chances of accessing it again in the future.

Make your touch exciting so she is curious about what more intense touching would feel like. Touching should rarely be static. If you have your arm around her, use your hand to touch, rub, or play with her neck or shoulders. If you're holding her hand, don't be limp and clammy – run your fingers lightly over her palm or the back of her hand.

16

IN THIS CHAPTER

Good dates, bad dates

A good date is one that advances your relationship goals. Figure out where you are in your emotional and physical progression, and structure your date to give yourself the best opportunity to move forward along both. Of course, much of the purpose of a date is to help your logistical progression – getting her alone, away from her friends, where you and her have the opportunity and time to get physical.

The ten principles below will help in most situations, but always start from an assessment of where you are with a woman and what you think you need to do to take it to the next level. Once you're clear on that, consider these 10 critical elements:

1. Planning

Never ask a woman what she wants to do on a date, at least not the first couple of times you go out with her. Have everything planned and prepared. Include backup plans if necessary. (If I'm taking a woman to an event that starts at a particular time and she's late or something unexpected happens, I always have a Plan B.) Being taken out is very attractive to a woman. I sometimes take this a step further and tell a woman, jokingly, that it's none of her business where we're going and that all she needs to know is what kind of shoes to wear.

2. Different

Plan something that she hasn't done over and over with men trying to be her boyfriend. They take her to dinner, they go for coffee, they meet for a drink, and if they're particularly inept, they invite her to the movies. These kinds of dates remind most women of the men they've rejected in the past, and are neither fresh nor interesting. If this is the best you can do, you won't seem fresh or interesting either.

3. External Stimulation

Take her where the environment is stimulating and where conversation isn't your primary source of entertainment. This is another problem with dinner, drinks, or coffee. Not only does this put a lot of pressure on your conversational skills, which can be a challenge if your skills aren't great yet or you don't know each other all that well, but your conversation will by necessity be mostly about abstract subjects instead of about the "here and now." That's fine most of the time, but over a two-hour dinner this can feel artificial, as though you are interviewing each other. When there is external entertainment and stimulation, it becomes much easier to be a good conversationalist. Think of going shopping or wine tasting instead of taking her for dinner and drinks.

4. Interaction

I have to add this one in case you go too far with the tip #3. Movies provide plenty of entertainment and things to talk about, but no opportunity for conversation or to learn about each other. What personality characteristics could either of you demonstrate at a movie theatre? That you know how to turn your cell phone off? That you eat popcorn? Make the date about a shared experience, not about a common experience enjoyed more-or-less independently.

5. Excitement

Take her through a range of sensations or emotions. For example, at a comedy club, she can be laughing, scandalized, or amused. Playing frisbee, she could be out of breath and excited. She could be entranced, offended, and visually stimulated at a gallery opening. Plan dates from the perspective of leading her through different emotions.

6. Your Turf

Invite her to come along to something you are already doing and knowledgeable about. You will naturally assume the powerful, dominant position. Contrast (A) – Her coming with you to your friend's exhibition at a gallery where you know the owner, with (B) – Your going out with her and her friends for drinks. In which scenario will it be easier for you to convey Status? In which scenario will all of her attention be on you, and where she will have to fight for yours?
In which scenario will she be more likely to feel jealousy?

7. Multiple Venues

Speed things up with multiple venues. Amusingly enough, this principle was the subtext of an episode of Sex and the City, a late 1990s TV show primarily directed at women. It feels like you've spent more time with someone and that you know them better if you've done lots of different things with them, even if each activity lasted only a short time. A date that starts with window shopping and then includes a bite to eat, browsing a bookstore, and a trip to a comedy club should make a woman feel like she's known you for a lot longer than just one date.

8. Logistics

Plan the logistics so that it's reasonable for her to come to your house (this is covered in more detail in Chapter 10 on Seduction). For example, pick activities near where you live. Or if you've been doing any physical activity, go home "to change." Or have her meet you at your place before you go out – that way her car will be there and you know that at some point you'll both need to return there.

9. Nights

If your aim is to move toward a sexual relationship, you should try to see her at night or plan dates that go into the evening. This is less of an issue if you've already had sex with her or if you're still early in the Comfort phase. Even though the human sex drive is actually highest in the afternoon, most people are culturally attuned to associate sex with nighttime. Wait until it's dark outside.

10. You

See her at a time when you'll be at your best. If you're tired and stressed on Tuesday afternoons because of your weekly meeting with your boss, don't do something right after work on Tuesday. Pick a time when you'll be feeling conversational, playful, and good about yourself, not tired and run down.

Good Dates Examples

The 10 principles not enough to get you started? Here are some more examples of good dates, but keep in mind that not all of these will be appropriate for all women (e.g., sporting events, shooting range):

Good Dates

Shopping	Concerts
Frisbee in the Park	Amusement Parks
Comedy Clubs	Picnics
Salsa Lessons	Shooting Range
Art Galleries	Cooking Classes
Sporting Events	Fireworks
Bicycling	Festivals
Wine Tasting	Sporting Events

How to date

Enjoy yourself at whatever activity you are doing. In most situations, the focus should be on the activity, not on her. You don't need to spend every second of the date with her. For example, if you are shopping, don't be afraid to wander around the store by yourself for a minute, and don't be affected if she does the same.

If there are other people you know in the same venue, talk with them. Introduce your date. The more you act as if the date is a big deal that requires you to change your behavior, the lower your social value will be for her.

Kissing and sexual escalation

Establishing the right frame early in your date is important. There is always a sub-text on a date of how far the two of you will go physically. Trust me, she's already thought about this and made some preliminary decisions before the date even started. Do not let the big tension on the date be about whether you are going to kiss at the end of the night. Get the kiss over with early, and then progress to other physical goals. This will help you later in the date, since neither of you will be thinking of kissing as a big deal or an uncertain issue. You'd rather a woman be wondering whether she wants her clothes to come off than whether she wants to kiss you.

Waiting until the end of the date and then going for the kiss is a weak move and will likely be typical of other men that she has dated and rejected. Make her think that you'll kiss her when you feel like it, not when you've run out of time and this is your last chance. Note that even if a woman was kissing you when you first met (i.e. at a bar), she may not respond to an immediate kiss on your first date. Touch immediately, but don't be surprised if re-establishing comfort with kissing you takes 15-30 minutes (or more).

I cover kissing in more detail in Chapter 19.

Paying for dates

It's gotten into some men's heads that by paying for a woman, they are "supplicating" or losing power. It's gotten into other men's heads that they need to impress a woman by taking her on an expensive extravaganza. Both perspectives are silly.

Here is all you need to know about money and dates:

- Don't use money to try to impress her.

- Don't let the bill cause awkwardness.

It is really that simple. Here's the underlying psychology:

If your first date with a woman involves something over the top, like a 5-star restaurant, she may instinctively feel that this is "too much." She'll wonder whether you are so lonely and so obviously not Pre-selected or Challenging that you're going all out for a woman that you don't know all that well and that money is all you have going for you. Or she'll be nervous that you feel – as some men do – that spending all this money on her makes you entitled to sleep with her.

Awkward situations affect women emotionally in a way that is incomprehensible to most men. Because you have no idea about her expectations – some women will offer to pay half, others will offer to pay but don't mean it, others will never offer – you are best off assuming that you're going to pay and planning accordingly. This has the additional bonus of showing her you can take care of her, which if done correctly should make her perceive you as dominant rather than supplicative.

Again, we're not talking about anything super-expensive. No sane woman is going to feel supplicated to if you bought two tickets to a comedy club and a couple drinks. More important is your attitude. Don't draw any attention to money or act like it's a big deal.

If you don't have very much money, then plan dates that don't require much money. It's that simple. There are plenty of free events on the list of good dates above.

If she offers to pay, she might just be offering out of politeness. Social convention implies that you should wave this off. If she offers again, or says something like "let me get this one" then let her contribute. Otherwise, you risk violating the second rule: don't let the bill cause awkwardness. But let her contribute in a way that still lets you be the leader. If she wants to chip in for drinks at a gallery opening, you can tell her she can buy you dessert afterwards. Now she's committed to going with you for dessert. This tactic is fun to play with, and you can use it to set up additional dates, with responses like: "I'll pay for this, and next week you can take me to that wine bar you were telling me about."

Volume 4 of the Love Systems Interview Series is a fantastic source of detailed and advanced techniques to make your dates more successful and prevent "flaking." Check it out in CD format (www.LoveSystems.com/CD4) or download it instantly (at www.LoveSystems.com/CB4) so you can start using these techniques right away.

Chapter 17: Storytelling

17

What is storytelling?

Storytelling is a crucial tool in your arsenal, especially in the Attraction and Comfort phases.

As discussed in Chapter 7, the Attraction phase is primarily about having a woman discover your positive characteristics. There are three ways to make this happen: she can Observe them; she can Learn about them from a third party; or she can be Told about them by you. Storytelling fits mostly into the third option as it allows you to tell a woman almost anything you want about yourself. It also provides an opportunity for her to Observe some of your good qualities – being a good storyteller and commanding a group's attention demonstrates Social Intuition and Status, and possibly Humor. It also shows her that you are able to feel and convey emotion.

Storytelling in the Comfort phase (Chapter 9) can help build a meaningful connection with a woman. Stories provide a great opportunity for her to get to know you better and should encourage her to tell you about herself as well.

What stories you tell and how you tell them gives a woman great insight into your personality. Make sure that your stories (and their delivery) reflect the best part of you, your values, and your identity.

I'll be using lots of mini-examples in this chapter. Often these won't be complete stories, or they will be exaggerated to make my point clear. Don't memorize and repeat them; most were created just for this chapter to illustrate one particular storytelling technique, and aren't designed to work well on their own. For hundreds and hundreds of complete stories that the masters use, check out the Love Systems Routines Manual at www.LoveSystems.com/Routines.

Storytelling structures can get pretty complicated, but they don't have to be. When I am telling stories, I focus on six key elements:

- A hook line

- The flow (main content of the story)

- Embedded information

- Opportunities for input

- Open threads

- A conclusion

Hook lines

A good hook line will introduce a story and give some clue about what's coming. It should create some suspense and anticipation to focus your listener's attention. Commanding attention is especially important in the Attraction phase, when you might be in a higher-energy environment and dealing with her and her friends. In the Comfort phase, attention is easier to get and you are more likely to be alone with her anyway.

A hook line can be a statement or a question. Some examples:

- Have you ever been to Paris?

- I just had the craziest day!

- You know, you remind me of…

In theory, the hook line should be related to the story you are going to tell. But it's better to have an interesting hook line that isn't completely related to the rest of the story than it is to have a perfectly on-message hook line that doesn't capture your listener's attention.

You can use the hook line as "bait," which is somewhat similar to using Open Threads (see below). Consider the following dialogue between two people who already know each other:

He: How are you?

She: Good, how are you?

He: Not bad. A bit tired; my plane was stuck on the runway for two hours this afternoon. I had to go to New York for the day [bait].

She: Why?

He: [Begin story about going to New York for the day.]

The flow

The main content of the story should flow naturally to a woman which means you are taking her on an emotional journey. Remove unnecessary logical or factual detail. You only want the minimum amount of non-emotional content to make your story make sense; additional detail must serve a specific purpose (e.g. rooting or embedding DHVs, as explained later in this chapter).

To give an example of how this is done, let's take a description of my recent trip to the East Coast and give it more of an emotional impact. For now, we're not worried about hook lines or anything else; we're just trying to replace facts with emotions.

Bad Storytelling:

I was in Philadelphia last week on business and when I was there, I went to visit a friend of mine in New Jersey. When I was there we went to all-you-can-eat-sushi night at this Japanese restaurant in Trenton. My friend has always been kind of cheap and loves to get a good deal, so even though he wanted the sashimi, he ordered the sushi because unlimited sushi was $25 but unlimited sashimi is $30. I guess the sushi is cheaper because the fish is the expensive ingredient so people will get full after eating less fish if they are also eating the sushi rice and the seaweed.

My friend's plan was to take the fish out of each sushi roll and send the rice and seaweed back. That way he'd get all the sashimi he'd want for $5 less. They told him to stop after his first plate but then he did it again a manager came out screaming at us and we had to leave. Fortunately, my friend paid for the dinner when we got kicked out and we decided that we didn't have to leave a tip.

Better Storytelling:

My friend just took me to all-you-can-eat sushi. Sushi is my favorite food so I was really excited. But my friend is really cheap and always loves to get a good deal, even if it makes things kind of awkward. He wanted sashimi but that costs more than all-you-can-eat sushi because with sushi you'll get full on the rice before you eat as much fish, and the fish is what's expensive.

So my friend ordered the sushi and ate the fish out of every roll and sent the rice back. This gave me that feeling of bad anticipation, you know that feeling you get in your gut when your best friend is about to totally embarrass himself... and you. Eventually, they caught on and the manager started screaming at us. I was embarrassed but also trying not to laugh; you know how that feels. I knew either my friend or the manager was being an idiot and I couldn't figure out which, but my friend paid for dinner, so I'm on his side.

You may actually prefer the first story to the second. This gives some insight into male vs. female communication as well as written vs. oral communication. The first story is logical and sequential; the second is more emotional. As such, the first "reads" better while the second "sounds" better.

You want to sound more like the narrator of the second story. It conveys more emotion. Neither story really conveys a lot about my personality or creates much of a connection – we're about to get into that – but the second example shows how you can make even a mundane experience seem emotionally-charged.

Embedded information

Embedding means using a story that appears to be about one subject to subtly tell listeners about something else. Usually the "something else" will be positive characteristics about yourself that you don't want to bring up directly because you don't want to come across as bragging or trying too hard to impress her.

Thus, what you are trying to communicate to her – usually a DHV, as discussed in Chapter 7 – is not the main point of the story. Consider this example:

I love New York, but I always thought there was something strange about the city. I think I know what it is now. It's mushrooms. I did a show there last week and afterwards a bunch of us went on a helicopter tour. It was really beautiful and all, but the weird thing was all the satellite dishes on the roofs. It was like a sea of little white patches, like the skyscrapers had all grown mold. So I figured it out. New York is strange because we're all living under giant mushrooms, just like the Smurfs.

Theoretically, the story is about how satellite dishes look like mushrooms from the sky. That's true by the way. It's amazing what you can learn from a Love Systems book. But the point of this story is the embedded DHVs:

1. The narrator does "shows" in New York, among other places. This implies Status, and potentially Wealth. In reality, it can be a trade show for all that it matters at this stage.

2. Helicopter rides are fairly routine for the narrator. To most women, this implies Wealth, and possibly Status. In fact, helicopter rides aren't all that expensive or a big deal; they just seem that way. Go take one so you can tell stories about it.

Create your own embedded DHV stories for the Attraction phase. Start by thinking of events or situations from your own life that relate to any of the attraction switches discussed in Chapter 3. Then, figure out a larger context in which you could tell a story in which that DHV would be an incidental detail, but would fit naturally within the story. "Larger context" here simply means that the story is about something bigger. In the example above, shows and helicopters are DHVs and fit into the larger context of "New York" or "why New York feels weird."

There are a virtually unlimited number of ways to embed different DHVs. To get you started, here are some phrases or lines that could fit into larger contexts and imply good things about you:

*   I took some friends on a rafting trip up north... (Health)

*   I had to talk my way out of that one... (Social Intuition)

*   I was sailing with some friends of mine... (Wealth, Status)

*   I'm sort of the leader of my peer group... (Status)

Embedding can backfire if you don't do it right. Here are the three most common embedding mistakes I've seen men make:

1. The embedded DHVs are out of place, or look forced into the story.

    > *"I was at the Ferrari dealership to get my car serviced, and my cell phone rang, and it was my brother, so I told him about what happened last weekend when I was doing a show in New York..."*

    This isn't subtle. There's nothing relevant about being at a car dealership, let alone about having a Ferrari in this story.

2. The story is uninteresting without the DHVs.

"I love New York. I had a show there last week and afterwards a bunch of us went on a helicopter tour. It was really beautiful, and I was surprised that I didn't have any fear of heights like I normally do."

A story about not being afraid of heights is not interesting. She'll know you only told the story because of the DHVs, which robs them of their power and conveys low Social Intuition.

3.   The DHVs overshadow the story.

"I love New York, but I always thought there was something strange about the city. I think I know what it is now. It's mushrooms. I was hanging out with my friend Donald Trump and he took us on a helicopter tour to check out some locations for a new casino we're building together. It was really beautiful and all, but the weird thing was all the satellite dishes on the roofs. It was like a sea of little white patches, like the skyscrapers had all grown mold. So I figured it out. New York is strange because we're all living under giant mushrooms, just like the Smurfs."

No one unintentionally includes details about building a casino with Donald Trump in a story about how satellite dishes look like mushrooms. Building a casino with Donald Trump is unambiguously much more important than how satellite dishes look, so it's simply not credible to tell a story about satellite dishes as if your casino plans were an incidental detail. The bigger the DHV, the bigger the story embedding it must be.

Open Threads

Another good advanced tactic is to leave open threads for your audience to ask about, to spur further conversation or to advance the story. For example, in the mushroom story, the phrase "I did a show there last week" is an open thread. She may ask you what you do for a living, or what kind of show you did in New York.

If you dropped hints about something that you don't want to get into details about, brush off her follow-up questions and create an air of mystery by saying "I don't want to talk about that now. Get to know me for me" and immediately start a new conversational subject. Run an opener if you don't know what to say next, but make sure there is no long awkward pause. Passing up easy opportunities to DHV in response to her questions can actually be a DHV in itself.

As an exercise, look for the open thread in this monologue:

> *I was in Japan last week and all over the place there are these machines that look like they sell soft drinks, but it's actually like 50 flavors of milk. Ever had strawberry milk? It tastes like a trip to the dentist. And you don't put coins in, either; you use your cell phone to dial a drink.*

The open thread would be; what was I doing in Japan?

Open threads are often used in Opening (Chapter 5) to set up your Transition (Chapter 6).

Opportunities for input

A story can have a more powerful effect on someone if they are actively engaged in it as opposed to just listening passively. Try to structure opportunities for a woman to feel that she is contributing to the conversation. This should be done carefully, as she might unpredictable derail the story's direction or create awkward moments by being unable or unwilling to contribute meaningfully.

In previous examples, we've been using elements of an Attraction story, so now we'll switch gears to Comfort. The story fragment we'll use is actually true and is about my mom's cat when I was a kid. Stories about childhood experiences are generally good in Comfort. They can make you seem vulnerable without being weak, they give you an opportunity to laugh at yourself, and they allow you to share commonalities. You'll notice that this story has no hook line; we'll add that in a moment.

Cat Story

My mom's cat was really old and really big. He was probably the only cat ever born without a sense of balance. I thought being able to balance on ledges and treetops was supposed to be part of the point of being a cat. But we lived on an island, so maybe we had mutants. Anyway, when I was little, my first memories are of him walking along the edge of my crib and losing his balance and falling on me. It scared me to death. It probably only happened once or twice, but in my memories it felt like it was happening all the time. In pre-school we all had to draw pictures of animals we were afraid of. The other kids drew snakes and monsters. Those never bothered me, not even when my older cousins tried to tell me there were snakes under my floor. I just laughed and told them I wasn't scared. No sir. What scared me was my mom's big old retarded cat. That's why today I have an aquarium. I'm pretty sure seahorses won't escape the tank and jump on me when I sleep.

This story could work fine on its own, if I added a hook line and a bit more emotional depth. But it could also be made better if a woman is actively engaged in it. The easiest way to create opportunities for input is to ask her questions about elements of your story that she might be able to relate to. For example:

- Did you have pets growing up?

- Do you like cats?

- What were you most afraid of when you were a kid?

Me: Did you have pets growing up?

Her: Yes, I had two dogs, a whale, and a llama. The llama's name was Bob. [Okay, she probably won't say this. When I'm creating sample dialogues, sometimes I have the woman say something ridiculous to emphasize that the exact content of her response is irrelevant to what I'm going to say next.]

Me: Oh yeah? My mom had a cat. And he hated me... Her: [Random response]

Me: My mom's cat was really old and really big. He was probably the only cat ever born without a sense of balance. I thought being able to balance on ledges and treetops was supposed to be part of the point of being a cat. But we lived on an island, so maybe we had mutants. Anyway, when I was little my first memories are of him walking along the edge of my crib and losing his balance and falling on me. It scared me to death. It probably only happened once or twice, but in my memories it felt like it was happening all the time. In pre-school we all had to draw pictures of things we were afraid of. What were you afraid of when you were little?

Her: [Random response – but this one will probably be really interesting and tell me a lot about her. Talking about this should build comfort. I can either pursue the conversation in this direction or leave it as an open thread from her and come back to it later.]

Me: The other kids drew snakes and monsters. Those never bothered me, not even when my older cousins tried to tell me there were snakes under my floor. I just laughed and told them I wasn't scared. No sir. What scared me was my mom's big old retarded cat. That's why today I have an aquarium. I'm pretty sure seahorses won't escape the tank and jump on me when I sleep.

Many opportunities for input are set up as questions. But they don't have to be. The dialogue below contains an example of a pause where the listener should feel compelled to contribute. I also make one of the opportunities for input into a hook line. This is often a good way of generating hook lines.

This story should have more of an impact on a woman than the first version, since she becomes invested, and contributes to it. The opportunities for input are not difficult for her, which is important. It's hard to be listening to someone else talk and then suddenly be put on the spot and have to come up with something interesting to say. But everyone knows what they were afraid of growing up and whether they had pets.

By the way, did you notice the open threads of "we lived on an island" and "I have an aquarium"?

Some general rules for inviting input:

- Make it as easy as possible for the listener.

- The listener's input should confirm or advance where the story is going anyway.

- Use "notional input" when you don't want to risk the story going in a different direction, or as training wheels to get practice as inviting input.

Notional input is where you ask her to confirm something that you assume to be true. For example, if you were telling a story about your nephew, you might start with "My 8-year old nephew Samuel did the funniest thing this morning. You like kids, right?" You wait for the "yes" answer and then continue with the rest of the story.

Conclusion

A good story should end on a high note that brings the action to a conclusion. It doesn't have to be a humorous punch line that leaves everyone rolling around in laughter, but it does have to wrap up the story and communicate that it is over. What you absolutely don't want is for someone to react to your story with an expectant pause and then say "so then what happened?" Here are some examples of good conclusions (you can imagine the stories that lead into them):

- "And that's why I never drink tequila".

- "I'm pretty sure he's never coming back".

- "That was probably the first time a kid had to tell his parents that THEY were grounded".

- "I'm pretty sure that seahorses won't escape the tank and jump on me when I sleep".

If you can't think of anything, you can finish by telling her what you learned from the experience. You don't have to actually say "and what I realized from this was..." although it's not bad if you do. In Comfort it might be a real lesson or insight. In Attraction it more likely should be something humorous.

Delivery

A story can take any length of time, from as little as 30 seconds to as long as 30 minutes, or even longer in the right context. Make your story length fit the situation. In a loud nightclub, no one is going to listen to you for more than a minute or two right after meeting you, so keep your stories short. Later on, when you're in the Comfort phase and maybe sitting in a quieter area, longer stories may be more appropriate. Learn to insert and remove material from your stories depending on the situation. Many of my best stories have a "short version" and a "long version." This is another reason why you should focus on the general outline of your stories as opposed to memorizing them word-for-word.

Make sure you get everyone's full attention before you begin. If you don't have the group's attention, either command it by being louder or stop talking until everyone is focused on you. If you lose someone's attention while you are telling them a story, just stop and look at them until they focus. Or you can playfully say: "hey, show's over here."

The biggest mistake I see most men make is that they are not "living the story." This is another reason why it's important that your stories are actually related to your personal experiences. For example, if you are telling a story about a party at your brother's house, you should be able to mentally immerse yourself in the atmosphere of the party. You should be able to see, smell, feel, hear, and taste everything that you were sensing at that moment.

Most of this information will be unnecessary detail. You may remember that your sister-in-law was wearing a long red dress that she looked uncomfortable in, but if it's not relevant to the story, don't include it. But you still need to know and feel these details to put yourself psychologically "in the moment." This will make your story much more captivating and seem more real. This is similar to how actors draw upon their personal experiences to convey attitudes and feelings and to create an emotional response in their audience. In addition, having that background detail available to you makes the rest of your storytelling better. This is similar to an author creating extensive "backstories" for his or her characters. The backstories are full of details that will never get into the book, but they endow the characters with much fuller and more interesting personalities.

If you're not interested in what you're talking about, there's no chance anyone else will be either. Take your new friends on a journey with you through the story. Personalize your openers, stories, and routines with things that you are genuinely passionate about. Someone with excitement and enthusiasm in his eyes talking about a model train set that he built (on the surface, not that fascinating to most women) will get far better results than someone going through the motions of talking about his career as a movie producer.

Insert pauses strategically in your stories. They create tension and anticipation. Using the stories we looked at previously in this chapter, I've added a couple of potential pauses. Often pauses will come while you're addressing facts as opposed to emotions:

- I love New York, but I always thought there was something strange about the city. I think I know what it is now. [pause] It's mushrooms. [pause] I did a show there last week and afterwards...

- My mom's cat was really old and really big. He was probably the only cat ever born [pause] without a sense of balance.

18

IN THIS CHAPTER

What is non-verbal communication?

Tonality

Body Language

What Is Non-verbal Communication? ("The Other 93%")

Many academic studies have emphasized the importance of non-verbal over verbal communication. An oft-quoted figure is that 93% of communication is non-verbal[8]. This is generally consistent with our experience.

Volumes have been written on non-verbal communication. Personally, I think a book, as a verbal medium, is an odd choice of format in which to teach a non-verbal process. That said, I'll cover the most important information here, but to perfect your tonality you need to hear it (and practice with someone who can hear you) and to perfect your body language you need to see it (and practice with someone who can see you). Some of the resources listed in Chapter 24, including audio and video products and downloads, provide further guidance, as do the in-famous Love Systems in-person workshops.

One of the good things about the techniques in this chapter is that they apply well beyond the dating world. Improving your non-verbal communication can help in many aspects of your social and professional life. Because of this, it's entirely normal to practice and ask for feedback on your non-verbal communication.

Non-verbal communication is generally thought of, in simplest terms, as tonality and body language.

Tonality

Tonality refers to how you say something, especially the volume, speed, and pitch of your voice.

Volume

Be louder. Most men at bars and nightclubs are too quiet, and it's extremely rare to see a sober man who is too loud. At first you may "lose your voice" from being louder. This is actually a good thing. Your vocal muscles are like any other muscles in the body; they become stronger after exertion and a recovery period. Deepening your pitch (see below) can also allow you to project your voice.

A commanding, confident voice is an extremely powerful tool. In contrast, a quiet or timid voice is as unattractive to women as a limp-wristed handshake. Early in an

---

[8] *Mele Koneya and Alton Barbour, Louder Than Words: Nonverbal Communication (Columbus, Ohio: Merrill, 1976)*

interaction, a woman should never have to strain to hear you or ask you to repeat yourself; if she does, that's a sure sign that you are not being loud enough. Later – once you get into the Comfort phase certainly – it's okay to make her lean in to hear you sometimes to build intimacy.

Don't let yourself get interrupted or talked over, especially by another man. If you're talking and someone else interrupts, keep talking until you finish your thought.

> Hint: You may feel uncomfortable at first speaking with a commanding, loud voice. Just because you feel that way doesn't mean it's too much. Often, at first, it's still not loud enough. Experiment and don't be afraid to push boundaries a bit to see where the line is, as far as volume goes.

Speed

Pace your delivery. Many men speak too quickly, especially when first meeting a woman. This suggests nervousness, as if you have to say your piece quickly before people stop paying attention. Adopt the attitude that you are interesting, that what you have to say is interesting, and that you are used to people listening to what you have to say.

Many men talk too quickly without realizing it. Consciously slow down your delivery in your next few interactions with women; you may be surprised by your improved results. In addition, by slowing down your speech, you will make it easier for others to understand you, especially in loud environments.

Pitch

Deepen your voice: As I mentioned in Chapter 5 on Opening, your voice should usually come from your chest, not from your throat. To try this out, put your hand on your chest, right below your pectorals, try to talk in two different ways: one in which you can feel the vibrations on your hand, and one where you can't. Consciously train yourself to speak in the way that you can feel the vibrations. That's your chest voice and it's what you should normally use to talk to women.

Variability

Use vocal modulation: Let your voice acquire a variable rhythm and tone. Use it to express emotion. If not, you will sound "flat" and have a difficult time retaining anyone's interest. Again, push "too far" in the direction of expressiveness. What at first feels like too much is often the right amount or even still not enough.

Body Language

Good body language is relaxed, calm, and confident. Bad body language is associated with (and usually comes from) insecurity, nervousness, and defensiveness.

As a general rule, if a position looks uncomfortable, it conveys low status. This is true whether or not a position happens to be comfortable for you. High-status men do not tend to squish themselves into awkward or uncomfortable positions.

Partly because of this, we endorse the principle of "locking in."

Locking In

Within the first 30-60 seconds of an interaction (longer in some specific cases, but shoot for this timeframe), you should be adopting a comfortable and socially-dominant physical position relative to the group you approach. This is especially true if the group is made up mostly of women, but it also applies to mixed groups as well.

The most common example of locking in comes when you are leaning up against a wall or a bar and the group is facing you.

This sounds harder to achieve than it is. Once you've been talking to a group for a few seconds, you can move around (or gently move the people you are speaking to) to establish this position. Just keep talking as if nothing is happening.

If the group doesn't happen to be near an appropriate vertical surface, you can wait a bit longer and then as you solidify the group's interest, you can slowly move and motion for the group to follow you, so that you establish this position.

Locking in also refers to sitting down with a group that is already seated. Deliver your false time constraint (see Chapter 5) as you sit. Use body language for the first couple minutes that you are sitting down to imply that you are about to leave.

Locking in is very important. If you stay standing next to seated group or face a group that has a wall behind it and you're obviously the outsider, you will lose value. Your physical positioning will imply that you are hitting on them, regardless of what you say. Not only will the group notice, but other people in the venue will notice. And you'll lose value with other groups you subsequently approach.

The following list highlights the most important body language dos and don'ts. But they don't all have the same importance. Focus first on everything in the head and face section (especially eye contact) and keeping your shoulders back. It's hard to simultaneously focus on 18 different things that your body is doing, especially while you're also trying to carry on a conversation. So focus on a couple of them at a time, internalize them until you don't have to consciously think about them, and then move on to the next ones.

Overall posture

- Don't lean forward to talk to someone. Tilt your head if you need to, but don't lean in so someone can hear you or so you can hear them. If you're having trouble being heard, speak up. If you can't hear someone, either carry on talking (before the Qualification phase) or suggest you move somewhere quieter (in the Qualification phase or subsequently).

- Don't slouch. Stand up straight. Sit straight. Not like a statue, you need to be relaxed a little bit, but don't hunch your shoulders or curve your back.

- Take up space. Within the boundaries of social politeness, don't be overly concerned about others' personal space. Men who are comfortable taking more physical space tend to be more attractive to women.

Head and face

- Eye contact is probably the most important element of body language. Hold eye contact 50% of the time when you are being spoken to and 90% of the time when you are speaking. If you are speaking to a group, switch eye contact between group members; at any given time, you should be making eye contact with one of them. At least early on, everyone in a group should get roughly equal attention; if anything, the woman you are interested in should get slightly less, not more. This helps make you a challenge to her.

- Keep your head up. Your neck should always be straight unless there is a specific reason to look down. This is a difficult one to internalize. Check yourself regularly. When I was learning to improve my body language, I focused on my head by doing a random spot-check every time I heard a phone ring.

- Relax your facial muscles, especially around your eyes and mouth. Go for a facial massage if you need to learn what relaxed facial muscles feel like.

- Smile. Show some teeth with your smile. Practice your smiles in front of the mirror. You should be smiling more often than not. Smiling actually releases positive brain chemicals, and this will help you develop a naturally positive and outgoing demeanor. And don't just smile with your mouth. The eyes are equally important and are the easiest way to tell between a fake and a real smile.

Chest and shoulders

- Keep your shoulders relaxed, down, and back. This is another difficult one to internalize and can also benefit from the "spot check" technique described above.

- When your shoulders are back, your chest should come out a bit. Don't puff up your chest any more than happens naturally through good shoulder positioning. That looks silly. Trust me, I tried this when I was starting out.

Legs and feet

- Keep your feet at least shoulder-width apart when you are standing.

- Allow your legs to take up a reasonable amount of space when sitting – don't curl your legs under you or do anything to minimize the physical space you occupy.

- When you're walking take big (but not ridiculous) steps but walk slower than normal. Your walk should communicate confidence and power. Imagine that you own the venue. Internalize this thought. Now walk. Feel the difference.

Arms and hands

- Don't fidget. Fidgeting implies nervousness and insecurity. If you tend to fidget, keep away from objects that may be problematic for you (pens, rings, napkins, etc.).

- Keep your hands out of your pockets.

- Don't make sudden wild gestures.

- Don't let your arms become a barrier between you and someone you are talking to (e.g., holding a drink between you).

- If you're like me and naturally have major problems making your hands behave themselves when you're in conversation, consider hooking one or both of your thumbs into belt loops of your pants or the top of your pockets.

- When you walk, keep your arms relaxed and to the sides of your body.

Chapter 19: Kissing

19

IN THIS CHAPTER

Implications of kissing

Sexual Attraction

Kissing and Sexual Tension

Kissing as an indicator

Kiss invitations

Implications of kissing

Kissing is a big deal. It's usually the first point in an interaction between you and a woman that is totally unambiguous. Anything verbal can be rationalized as "flirting" or "teasing." Non-sexual touching before kissing can be interpreted as "friendly" or "playful." However, kissing is usually the bright red dividing line between "friends" and "romance." Once you kiss someone, it's harder to rationalize this away or go backwards.

On one hand, this is good because it clearly advances the relationship. However, when you kiss, you risk dissipating the sexual tension that you'd built up with her.

To understand this, we need to take a detour through how sexual attraction works.

Sexual Attraction

Many variables affect sexual attraction and sexual behavior. The crucial one that many men miss – as it applies to female sexuality – is sexual tension..

Tension is crucial. It reflects the thrill of the chase. Even though you might be happy to have sex with a supermodel who spontaneously appeared on your bed, it is likely that you would want her even more if she appeared in your living room, and flirted with you, let your mind spend hours imagining having sex with her before you finally won her over. This buildup of anticipation and sexual tension can be important for men, but is crucial for most women.

To use another analogy, male sexual behavior is like an on/off switch, based primarily on a woman's looks. In contrast, female sexual behavior is like a pot of water on a hot stove, building up in intensity until her emotions reach a boiling point. This is true despite the fact that it takes about the same time (based on body chemistry) for men and women to become sexually aroused.

Kissing and Sexual Tension

When you and a woman are flirting and connecting, she will often start imagining or anticipating the kiss. She'll be wondering if you're a good kisser. And so on. That tension and ambiguity is fun and exciting for her. It keeps her interested. Once you kiss her, that ambiguity and tension can dissipate.

Have you ever known someone for a while where there was unspoken attraction between you two... but when you finally hooked up with her, it felt like you both "got that out of your system" and could go back to being friends instead of feeling like it was the beginning of a sexual relationship? That's because the anticipation and tension were gone. This can happen, especially for women, with kissing. We saw an example of this in the stories in Chapter 12: Social Circle.

To avoid this letdown, make sure that:

1)   The kiss is a good one.

2)   You immediately re-establish the tension.

How to be a good kisser is outside the scope of this book. Check out the Love Systems' product on Advanced Sexual Tactics, coming later this year. In the meantime, there's some decent stuff on The Attraction Forums, which is free (www.TheAttractionForums.com).

Re-establishing sexual tension

You can re-establish sexual tension either for more kissing or for more intense sexual touching. Generally, if you are in public or in a place where you could not realistically have sex, create anticipation for more kissing. If you're somewhere you could have sex, create tension for that.

- To create tension for more kissing:

- End the kiss first (but not too early).

- Playfully call her a bad girl, and tell her that's all she gets... for now.

- Create physical tension. Touch her face. Bring your lips close to hers while you are talking, but don't let her kiss you. Whisper in her ear, etc... You get the idea.

To create tension for sexual escalation:

- Make the kissing session long. Unless you sense that she is already "ready," kissing her for one minute and then feeling her up could be perceived as "too fast" and create a state break (see Chapter 10). Make out with her for 10+ minutes, and her body will start anticipating the next step.

- Kiss, but do more than kiss, so she anticipates the next step. Run your hands through her hair or pull it if you know how – there's an art to this. Grab her hair at the roots as low as you can on her neck. Pull firmly but gently downward. It takes practice. Kiss her neck, etc.

- Tease her physically. Run your hand up her leg, but pull it away before you get too high. Make sure you pull your hand away before she does, and make sure you are clearly teasing her and not merely "respecting her boundaries." Verbalize this.

Kissing as an indicator

Just because kissing is the first unambiguous test of whether you and she are sexually interested in each other, it does not mean that kissing should be used as a test or a confirmation of her attraction to you.

Have you ever been on a date with a woman and leaned in for that first kiss at the end of the night when she's saying goodbye on her doorstep?

This is a phenomenally weak move.

It says to a woman, "I'm interested in you; now I want to re-assure myself that you are interested in me." A confident man is accustomed to women being interested in him and kisses on his own schedule, not according to what he sees men do on TV. If it doesn't fit into your plan to kiss her then and there... don't. Try to make your first kiss at a moment when she hits an emotional high point in your interaction with her. Or to reward her for doing something you like.

Never kiss a woman to find out if she's interested in you sexually. Use the knowledge from this book and the social intuition you will develop from using it repeatedly to develop a sense of when a woman is interested.

Kiss Invitations

Personally, I just make the kiss happen. Once you have interacted with thousands of women, you will generally know when the opportunity to kiss becomes available. But if not, there are a bunch of "kiss routines" that set a woman up for that first makeout. There is a whole section of the Love Systems Routines Manual (www.LoveSystems.com/Routines) devoted to this. I'll include some examples here.

The Question Game Kiss

This routine was first invented by Mystery as an all-purpose kiss tactic. As a matter of preference, we tend to use this only as part of the Question Game (see Chapter 9). However, it can work in other situations too – try it with our other kiss invitations and see which you like the best.

What we do is ask, "Do you want to kiss me?" It's important to get the phrasing right. It's not "May I kiss you?" or "Are you going to kiss me?" The neutral phrasing is important.

Her likely responses can be divided into three categories:

1. **Green Light**. Responses here include "yes," "maybe," or leaning in to kiss you.

If you get any response like this, kiss her. If she says "maybe," respond with "let's find out" while you move to kiss her.

2. **Yellow Light**. Responses here include "not here" or "not yet."

She does want to kiss you, but not in this particular situation. Don't discuss. Don't try to solve her objections by moving somewhere else or arguing that you've known each other long enough. Just say "I understand" and let the conversation continue on another topic. Your opportunity will come up again later.

3. **Red Light**. Responses here include the ever-popular "no."

She is likely not interested in you yet. Or you have taken her by surprise and this was her instinctive reaction. Or she is interested in you but doesn't want to seem easy. Or she really meant *"not here"* or *"not yet."* If you get a rejection here, don't be negative. Just say something like *"I didn't say you could; it just looked like you had something on your mind"* and change the subject. You may need to add more Attraction, more Qualification, or more Comfort. Or elements of all three.

The "I'm trying to so hard not to kiss you" Kiss

This routine was first developed by Style as part of his Evolution Phase Shift routine. The part that is specifically necessary for kissing is to lean into her, smell her neck, and say:

"You smell so damn good. I'm trying so hard not to kiss you right now."

If she flinches, pulls back, or says something negative, then she is not likely to be receptive to a kiss. In this case, just change the subject and realize that you still have more work to do, similar to the "red light" scenario in the previous example. If she holds steady, leans in, or touches you, she is ready to be kissed.

The Almost Kiss

This appears to have been developed independently by Future and by Brad P. They have slightly different versions, so I will arbitrarily combine them with my own elements thrown in.

Say to her: *"I don't know if we're ready for a kiss yet, but I think we're ready for an almost kiss. I want you to be good and not take advantage of this an opportunity to kiss me. I just want you to hold still, sit on your hands, and you can get close but we can't kiss."*

Bring yourself very close to her lips (this is another reminder to always have good breath) but don't kiss her or make her think that you are trying to kiss her. Let some tension build for a couple of seconds and then pull away.

In a few minutes, you can say *"I think we're ready for another almost kiss."* Do the same thing. She will more than likely kiss you. If not, try again in another few minutes.

It's never taken me more than 3 times to get a kiss this way.

Chapter 20: Fashion & Grooming

20

IN THIS CHAPTER

Being good-looking

Conveying your identity

Putting an outfit together

Shoes and boots

Pants

Shirts

Accessories

Grooming

Being good-looking

Want some good news?

You can be good-looking enough for virtually any woman, without too much work.

This is because, for a man, being good-looking has far more to do with how you dress than it does with what you look like naked.

The bad news is that being good-looking will not usually do much for you by itself (women do reject men based on appearance, although not anywhere remotely near as often as men reject women for the same reason). Usually all it will do for you is prevent you from being rejected on the grounds of looks alone. Good looks can also give you more approach invitations (see Chapter 5), and give you more freedom overall to make mistakes. So you may as well do everything you can to improve them.

We certainly do. But don't expect this to change your life.

Another piece of bad news is that there is only so much "universal" advice about fashion and grooming that can apply to all men. I'd rather tell you this upfront than pretend that there is a magic formula that can bring out the best in everyone. To make the most out of your looks, get in-person advice from someone who can see what styles and outfits look best on you and knows what he's doing. This is one reason why our fashion consultations and Love Systems bootcamps (which usually include fashion consultations) are so popular. On the subject, I should say that relying too much on the advice of your female friends can be a mistake, unless they know what they are doing. In general, women have a tendency to suggest that men dress "nice" or like Barbie's boyfriend Ken, as opposed to in a unique way that will capture the attention and curiosity of other women.

This chapter will give you plenty of dos and don'ts to get you started, and over time you can and should develop a fashion sense yourself. Read GQ and Details (fashion-oriented magazines targeted at men) to get ideas. Look at what high-status men are wearing when you're out. Watch women who interest you and look at the fashion and grooming choices of the men they date. Then look at what the lonely men by themselves are wearing. Not only will this education process help you make the most of your looks, but it will also give you something interesting to talk about with women. Most women are interested in fashion and people-watching.

Consider yourself lucky that you are a man. It's relatively easy to improve your looks and most women aren't dead set on dating male models. Women who aren't physically attractive have a much harder time finding and keeping a desirable man.

Conveying your identity

Fashion and grooming serves a dual purpose. They do more than change your looks; they also project an identity.

Here's a thought-experiment. Imagine that you are visiting a big city that you're unfamiliar with. One night, you go out alone but you make a wrong turn and find yourself completely lost. You need to ask for help. You go to an intersection and see three different people, one on each of the other corners:

1.   A man in a well-fitted suit with clean shoes, a briefcase, and a fashion-able tie.

2.   A man in ripped pants sliding well below the waist, big boots with metal spikes, a bandana and a leather jacket.

3.   A man dressed in shorts, sandals, and an oversized wool sweater.

Don't read on until you visualize and think about how you feel about each of them and which of them you'd ask for help.

When you imagined these people, did their clothing choices lead you to make assumptions about each of them? Keep in mind that I didn't tell you anything about them – I just said it was "a man" each time. But if you're like most people, you inferred other things about them based on their clothes. You might even have inferred physical characteristics. Was one man big, while another was small? Did they vary in strength? Were they of different races?

Let's dig deeper. The first man probably didn't scare you because he so obviously belonged in a corporate environment. You can guess what kind of job he might have, what kind of place he works in, what kind of things he does on his free time, and so on. You might be wrong because individual people do defy patterns, but you'd be right most of the time. This is because you've met men who dress like this in the past or seen them on TV and in the movies, and you've learned about personality traits that such men often have in common.

The second man probably scared you. He's dressed like we expect someone who was violent might dress if he were going to be in a dark alley. Even if we don't know any muggers personally, we have an idea of what we think they look like from the media.

The third man probably scared you too, for a different reason. He might be crazy or otherwise mentally unbalanced. The informal rules of our society tell us not to wear outfits like that, so this is someone who doesn't accept societal rules. Logically, if it's warm enough for sandals and shorts, it's too warm for a sweater.

The purpose of this was to put you inside a woman's head. Remember, when you first start interacting with her, she won't know much about you, and your clothes are one of her most useful sources of information:

- She knows that your clothes didn't fall on you by accident. You made a choice to wear what you're wearing and she will use that information to make assumptions about you.

- She will make implicit assumptions about you without even realizing it. Before she even really notices you, she may already think you are "boring" or "sexy" or "creative."

- She is going to assume that you behave and live a lifestyle similar to those of other men she has met who dress in a similar way.

- She is going to draw on stereotypes from the media, especially films and television, and assume that you emulate, or are trying to emulate, movie or TV characters who dress that way.

So, how you dress is important not only for enhancing your looks but also for conveying your identity. She's going to make judgments about you based on your clothes anyway, so you may as well have her make the judgments you want. This is another reason why one-size-fits-all fashion and grooming advice can be a disservice.

With that in mind, let's look at some of the general rules that actually do apply to most men.

Putting an outfit together

- Each outfit should have some basics (pieces which do not obviously attract attention) and some artistry (pieces which do attract attention). For example, if your shoes and jacket are a bit flashy or edgy my preferred look then stick to relatively subdued pants and shirt. Depending on your overall look, the artistry can be very subtle or very dramatic.

- "Peacocking," or wearing extremely ridiculous and out-of-place outfits is outdated. Dress to attract some attention, but make sure what you're wearing fits together, supports your identity, and doesn't look ridiculous. Peacocking will attract a lot of attention, but it's mostly surface-level curiosity and entertainment.

- Make your clothes fit – why spend $80 on a great shirt that doesn't fit if you won't spend $5-$10 to have it altered? If it doesn't fit you perfectly, get it altered so it flatters your body.

- Speaking of fit, while I don't generally suggest that you rely on women's advice for how to dress, one thing most women are very good at is helping you find clothes that fit well. As long as you're prepared to disagree with her about what styles to wear, take a woman shopping with you to help judge the fit. Alternatively, if you're shopping alone, ask other women whether something you're trying on fits you well. You can use this to start a conversation as well – it's not a great opener, but if your primary goal at the time is shopping, then any women you meet will be a bonus.

- Suits are often very attractive if you can justify wearing them. Don't be afraid to wear a suit to a nightclub with your friends. Be more afraid to wear one to a dive bar. Either way, take off or loosen your tie and unbutton the top button of your shirt.

- Don't be boring. If you dress just like everyone else, she will assume you are just like everyone else. Which would be a big waste after you've read this book and learned how to stand out from the pack.

- If you're overweight, black clothes make you look thinner. If you're short, pinstripes make you look taller (and horizontal stripes make you look shorter). If you have a nice body, show it off with your clothes, but not too much – clothes that are too tight might make her think you're gay.

- Don't clash. Don't wear two different patterns in the same outfit. Don't wear two different stripes (including pinstripes). Colors that are too close together can often clash (like black and navy blue, or white and cream). Red and green also don't tend to work well together; neither do black and brown. If you know what you're doing, you can break all of these rules, but hopefully not all in the same outfit.

Shoes and boots

- Be taller – There are plenty of brands of very fashionable shoes and boots that give you extra height. A couple extra inches will always help. If you're under six feet (about 180 cm), a couple extra inches will help a lot.

- Creativity matters with shoes. Women really notice shoes, which is why it's important that they be stylish and clean. It's a rare man who wears anything other than traditionally boring footwear. You can stand out through your choices here.

- Don't wear the same shoes two days in a row. This isn't a fashion tip; it just makes your shoes last much longer.

Pants

- Designer jeans are fashionable these days, khakis less so. Generic boring cotton pants are death.

- The fit of a pair of jeans is very important. Different brands and styles are cut in different ways. Make sure you know what you're doing; don't just guess. Expensive jeans are expensive because of the cut. It's usually worth investing in designer jeans.

- If you're going to the park or the beach and you want to wear shorts, make sure they are loose and come pretty close to your knees. Nothing will get you laughed at more quickly than tight shorts. Avoid shorts outside of physical activity.

Shirts

- Keep informal collared shirts outside your pants; don't tuck them in.

- Wear collared shirts alone, without a t-shirt underneath. Only wear a t-shirt if you sweat a lot.

- Short-sleeve button-down shirts are often boring and ugly.

- Shirts give you a lot of room for subtlety and creativity. You should almost never wear a plain, solid-colored, collared shirt unless the color itself is unique. Even if for whatever reason you are dead set on wearing a plain white shirt, you can give it an intriguing touch with a bit of texture, subtle patterns, or French cuffs.

Accessories

- Get some ornamental stuff -- Earrings, funky shoes, rings, hats, scarves, neck-chains, wristbands, whatever. What is purely ornamental (e.g., a double breasted suit, cuff links, jewelry) is sexy. What is purely functional generally is not. Don't go overboard – one or two ornamental elements is usually enough. Women will often ask you about these, so it's even better if you have a good story behind them. In this way they can function as physical "open threads" (see Chapter 18: Storytelling). Women often notice accessories and it's an easy way to convey that you have a sense of style.

- Glasses – Glasses are sexy on some men. They are not on most men. If you look better without them, try contacts or surgery.

- Unless you know what you are doing, match your shoes to your belt (i.e., make them both brown or both black).

- Have an interesting belt buckle. It doesn't have to be over-the-top – elegant is also interesting.

Grooming

- This may be obvious, but better safe than sorry. Remove excess hair -- If your eyebrows are even close to touching, wax or shave them so there is separation. Nose and ear hairs are sexy to no one. If you have sideburns, make sure they end in a neat line at the bottom and are the same length on each side. Hair should not be found on your back or butt. And while we're at it, your pubic hair shouldn't be unruly either. Women will appreciate your privates being trimmed and neat and may be more enthusiastic about rewarding you for this.

- If you have a beard or a mustache, keep it trimmed and neat. Most of the men I see with beards or mustaches should shave them off anyway, though they do look good on some people. Having 3-day stubble on your face can be attractive on some men; keep this orderly as well and don't let any hairs get too long.

- Women's preferences vary widely here and can be somewhat random. Don't take any individual woman's advice too seriously on this. But if you ask ten women what they think of your mustache and they all hate it, get rid of it.

- Squelch acne -- First, if you're still getting acne, see a dermatologist. Second, for your acne scars, consider laser skin care (expensive) or makeup (cheap). Get a female friend to help you buy a cover up stick and some powder. You can make your zits vanish for the night. No excuses here. Unless you have a particular skin condition, acne can and should be minimized.

- Whiten your teeth -- It's cheap and easy. Go through your dentist, not those white strips. No excuses here either.

- A good haircut makes a major difference. Find people with attractive haircuts and ask who they go to. It's absolutely worth spending the money on a good haircut. If your budget is tight, you may only have to do this once, to establish the cut, and then every month or so you can go to someone cheaper but technically competent and ask him or her to keep trimming your hair in the same style.

Just a few changes can make a big difference. Take a look at these before-and-after pictures of Masters, a retired instructor (and former computer geek). Notice the big difference that a fashionable haircut, an edgy/stylish element (the light sunglasses), and a sharp blazer can make.

Before   **After**

OK, now relax. Have you done all the things in the list? You've done the best you can with what you have. Women will notice. An average-looking man who takes care of himself is often more attractive to women than a better-looking man who is a slob. Whatever you are able to do, remember that looks are neither a necessary nor sufficient condition to attract most women. Just take control of the message you are conveying through your wardrobe and make sure you've put your best foot forward.

Chapter 21: Winging

21

The term "wing" or "wingman" comes from military aviation. The pilot flying just outside and behind the squadron leader is flying on the leader's wing, making him the leader's wingman. In popular culture, the wingman is a man who helps his male friend meet women, usually by engaging her friends and often by making a romantic connection himself.

The most important thing is to work with your wing, not against him. Your friends should never be your competition. If you and your friends are tripping each other up or fighting each other for women, people can assume a few things about you:

> You don't have much going for you. If you did, you wouldn't spend time with people that you don't seem to like and respect, and/or who don't seem to like and respect you. This implies that you have low Status (see Chapter 3).
>
> You don't have many friends. For the same reason as above, and with the same implications – that you have low Status.
>
> You don't have much success with women. If you did, you wouldn't fight one of your friends for a woman you just met. This implies that you are not Pre-selected (Chapter 3).

The big message here is that people will make judgments about you based on your friends and how you interact with them.

Successful men normally spend time with other successful people. If you're at a restaurant with Brad Pitt, many women will want to meet you. Even if they have no chance at Brad (Angelina is pretty tough competition), they'll be curious about someone who has enough going for him that Brat Pitt counts him among his friends. On the other hand, if your companion is a generic-looking accountant who is wearing khakis, a tucked in shirt, and nothing stylish or adventurous, women will be far less interested in you. Even though you haven't changed, women's perceptions of you will, as they infer things about you, your friends, and your lifestyle.

You want your friends to have value. Never cut them down. Act around them as if they are movie stars who are also your good friends – like it's totally normal for you to be hanging out with very high-value people.

Of course, it's not enough to tell you what you do; you need to know how.

Here are some specific ways you and your friends can make each other look great.

- Only one of you should approach a particular group. If you approach, your friend should wait a couple of minutes and then see if you want him in the group. Generally, you will – for reasons discussed above. However, there are situations where you won't. For example, if you entered a group of three people and you were about to pull one of the women away for a more private conversation (see Chapter 9), adding your friend at this point could be awkward and unnecessary. If you go out with your friends a lot, this communication can become instinctive. Whatever you do, keep it simple. You don't want a complicated sequence of password phrases. If I'm out with someone new, I will tell him that the keyword is "Tanya." If either of you mention Tanya when the other one is about to join the group, it means "go away."

- Introduce your friends properly. If I'm out with Tenmagnet, I won't say

  "Hey, this is my friend Tenmagnet." (For one thing, I'd use his real name.) I'd tell people: "This is my friend Tenmagnet. He's an amazing musician and he's kicking ass at law school too. You should have seen his show at The Diamond last week. I'd roll with him anywhere."

Building up your friends when they are not around has much more of an effect than when they are around. So try to talk about "who you're here with" before your friends join you in the group. When they do, women will often already be attracted to them. These are Learned DHVs (biased source) from Chapter 3.

- Give priority to your friend. If you are the first into a group and your friend appears a few minutes later, turn to face him. Address him. He is automatically more important than any woman you've been talking to for a few minutes. Similarly, if a woman later makes fun of your friend, roll your eyes at her. When your wingman teases her back, laugh and nod your head.

- Talk to each other. If a friend and I meet two women, we will still spend a significant amount of time talking to each other, even when the women are around. This implies that you have a solid social circle (Status) and that your attention has not been completely won by the women (Challenging). You can even talk with your friends about the women you've just met - it's a great opportunity to tease them or to introduce a venue change. For a venue change, I might say something like:

  "I'm hungry, let's go get sushi."

If my wing is on the ball, he'll agree. Then one of us will turn to the women and say:

> *"Hey, you guys should tag along. We're going to my friend's restaurant; they have killer sake you've got to try."*

At that point, assume they are coming, take them by the hand, and go.

- Give your friend a boost. If I'm out with a friend and it's going well for me but not for him, I can help him out. I will often say something to "my" woman like:

    > *"I'd love to stay and talk. I'm really curious about you. But your friend is being weird to my friend and I don't want him to get bored."*

Usually "my" woman will elbow her friend / "his" woman in the ribs or something to tell her to be nicer to my friend. Continue from there.

- Progress physically in sync with your wing. Women don't like their friends to think that they are "easy." But "easy" is a relative, not objective, standard. If two women meet two men, whichever woman sleeps with her guy first is the easy one, whether it's in 3 hours or 3 days or 3 months. So, if you and a friend meet two women and take them home, separate them so they can't see each other. Then escalate. Make a lot of noise so it's obvious to the other couple that you are getting physical. Then your friend's woman won't feel cheap if she lets him escalate. Then he will make sure they make noise, so your woman feels reassured.

- Respect "the rules." Whoever is the first man to approach a group gets to choose the woman he wants to attract. No exceptions. Sometimes you need to talk to the less interesting woman for an hour to give your friend the time to succeed with his woman. He'll do the same for you. Trust me, once you get good at this, you'll realize that there are more than enough beautiful women to go around.

Chapter 22: Phone Game

22

IN THIS CHAPTER

Phone Game

Most phone game takes place in the Comfort phase (see Chapter 9). However, you need to think about phone game differently from regular, in-person comfort building. This is partly because one of the major purposes and challenges of being on the phone with a woman is to arrange for the two of you to actually meet up in person again.

In addition, the nature of your interaction is different on the phone. You can't see each other's body language. You can prepare much better. Neither of you actually has to answer the phone. Most people have Caller ID. Conversations can end with very little notice. And so on. We'll analyze the impact of these factors in this chapter.

The Goal of phone game

As stated above, your primary aim with Phone Game is to get her to meet up for a date. Your secondary aim is to use time on the phone with her to build comfort. Of course, you'd build far more comfort in person than on the phone over an equivalent time period; however, until you can see her again in person, the telephone is your best tool to move the relationship forward.

Script the call out beforehand and write down some notes. Why not? She can't see you. Plan the first couple of things you are going to say and a couple of things you can jump in with if you run out of things to say. Uncomfortable silences on the phone are deadlier than they are in person, since a phone conversation – or a relationship – can end after just a few awkward seconds, when she says, "Well, I have to go now."

How to get her phone number

This is actually the wrong question to start with. The right question is: why should you get her number? It's so you can go on a date with her. A phone number has no value in itself. For that matter, neither does a date. There is nothing in the Emotional Progression Model that mandates meeting her again at a different time – which is all a date really is – rather than continuing forward at that moment.

In a way, trying for a date is an admission of failure, even if most of the time it's an unavoidable "failure." Trying to meet up with her later says: "I am not trying to move this relationship forward right now. I am going to try to continue this later. In the best case, I'd be right where I am now. In the worst case, we won't end up meeting up and I lose the relationship with her."

A date never gains you anything. All it does is give you another chance to push the relationship forward if the logistics weren't right to do so when you met her. Of course, most of the time, the logistics won't be right when you first meet. If you meet a woman on your lunch break and you have to get back to work, you'll need to set up a date. If she's shopping with her girlfriends and can't leave them, you'll need to set up a date. If you're both at a club but it would be socially awkward for you to leave together, you'll need to set up a date.

But remember – a date is not a phone number. A phone number is a chance at a date. There's still a chance that she will flake (not answer or return your call, not go on a date with you, etc.)

Here's a true story from a recent Love Systems' workshop in Los Angeles: We took the guys to a lounge in Hollywood and one of them was deep in conversation with Suzanne, a very fit Asian woman. Suzanne's friends were happy for her to talk to our guy because he had already won them over in Attraction and Comfort (as per the Emotional Progression Model). It was about midnight. There was no time pressure. But when our student "ran out of things to say" he took her phone number and rejoined us.

This was a bad decision. Leaving aside that you should never run out of things to say, all that the phone number was going to accomplish was to help them meet up again to spend time together. However, they were already in the middle of spending time together without any obvious barriers to developing their relationship.

Our student wasn't lazy. His motivations are understandable. Psychologically, he wanted to "lock in" what he had "gained" so far: her willingness to give him her phone number. But that's a rookie mistake.

Of course, we didn't let him leave Suzanne. We led him back to her with instructions to escalate until rejection. When the lights came on an hour later, they left to get pizza, and then went home together. There was no need for a date or a phone number. Of course, it doesn't always work so easily, but it will never work if you don't try.

Our student made dozens of mistakes with Suzanne. We were watching him the whole time and went over them the next day. However, because he didn't settle for a phone number and risk being forgotten, because he did enough things right, he got the girl.

Women and "flaking" – How not to get her number

Why does flaking happen? Let's look at an example of a typical, attractive, social woman.

She goes out to a restaurant with her friends. While waiting at the bar, an interesting man approaches her. 3 to 5 minutes later (about how long it should take to get some attraction going), he asks for her number so they can "hang out sometime." At that moment, she genuinely would "hang out" with this man "sometime"...

...but it doesn't turn out that way.

Going out "sometime" is different from going out Thursday night. To see her "sometime" all you have to do is be more interesting than doing nothing. That's a pretty low standard. She can agree to that. And, if she has nothing else to do, she might actually see you. However, most desirable women rarely have "nothing else to do."

Thus, to see her at a specific time, you need to be more interesting than anything else she could be doing, like friends, hobbies, work, other dates, or relaxing at home. That's a tough standard to meet in 3-5 minutes. Especially since over the course of the night she met a bunch of other men. Did you think you were the only man to notice her? She likes all of the attention and flirting, but she doesn't have time to go on 9 dates this week.

Bear this in mind: meeting up with strange men is scary for most women. First, there are issues of physical safety. If she's not comfortable with you, she may feel the risk of date rape or worse. Less dramatically is the hyper-developed fear that many women have of being in awkward social situations.
What if she isn't attracted to you when she sees you again?

A woman is going to look for reasons NOT to go out with you.

To a man, the idea that you might not have a great time with this woman is irrelevant; maybe you will, maybe you won't. Either way, you'll never know if you don't meet up, and the worst thing that can happen is you'll cut it short early and go home. Men don't agonize and worry over whether it will be socially awkward or not. But many women do, and we need to take this into account.

Women also tend to be more analytical than men about social situations. She may wonder why you'd even call her when you only met for a few minutes and you know so little about her (after all, you spent that time attracting her as opposed to learning about her). Are you desperate? Or are you a player?

It should be clear by now that a quick interaction leading to some basic attraction and "we should hang out sometime" is rarely going to lead an exceptionally desirable woman into seeing you again. She fears loss of safety, she fears social awkwardness, and who are you anyway?

How to get her phone number – for real

To have a good chance of seeing her again, you need to establish some comfort with her during the first interaction. This means you need to open, transition, attract, and qualify her first. I don't care if you only have 10 minutes. You just have to play faster.

Here are some anti-flaking tactics for getting her phone number:

Have something specific to do. She should plan to help you shop for your niece's birthday on Saturday, not "hang out sometime."

- Bait her into suggesting the date. Let her chase you. Drop little hints ("I'm going to X" or "I'd love to do Y") and see if she tries to become part of those plans or says something like, "That sounds fun; I'd love to do something like that."

- Don't make the date, or the phone number exchange, the last part of your interaction. That feels like a pickup. Stay at least 5 minutes afterwards.

- Engage her friends. When she goes home, her friends should be excited for her that you guys are meeting up later and not wondering who that creepy guy was. To a woman, her friends' approval for the men she dates is very important, much more important than peer group approval is for men. See Chapter 9 on Comfort for more on this.

- Focus on the date, not the phone number. The phone should be an afterthought (and isn't always strictly necessary, although you take a big risk that she won't think your plans are serious if you don't get her number).

- Set up callback humor. If you have a running joke during your interaction where you have a nickname for her, and later you phone her and call her by that nickname, it often triggers a reversal to the previous emotional state. She'll be back in the world of being out, having fun, and meeting men, as opposed to whatever mundane thing she was actually doing when you called.

- Program your number into her phone. Many people will not answer the phone if they don't know who is calling. This way she'll know, for better or worse, that it's you. Set up more callback humor by having her program your name as "My hero" or "Mr. T" or whatever is playfully relevant.

- If she's drinking, address it. Tease her that she won't remember anything because she's drunk. Pretend that you guys would have so much fun together, but she had to ruin it by being drunk and making it so it would be weird when you call. Bait her into convincing you that she's not all that drunk, that she's really into you, and she can't wait to hear from you. After she's said that, it becomes a lot harder for her to be flaky. Warning, don't do this unless the woman actually IS really drunk. It will annoy her if she's just had a drink or two.

- If she is strongly interested in you, tell her exactly when you will call. Get her to promise to answer. But don't make this sound too serious.

Making plans: men vs. women

I stated above that the primary goal of phone game is to go on a date with her. That doesn't mean that you should approach phone calls with a "I'm trying to make plans" frame (see the Glossary for a definition of "frames"). You'll seem desperate and typical of low-status men.

Men and women tend to view the telephone differently. Men see the phone as a tool that allows us to schedule our lives and arrange meet-ups with friends. In other words we use the phone to get things done. Women see the phone as a source of conversational pleasure and connection. Do you recognize this type of conversation?

Man 1: Hi, Man 2.

Man 2: Hi, Man 1. What's new?

Man 1: There's a new Spanish restaurant on Chestnut Street. Do you want to check it out?

Man 2: Sure. Tomorrow?

Man 1: Can't. I'm swamped this week. Next Monday?

Man 2: Perfect. Around 8?

Man 1: That works. I'll make reservations for 8.

Man 2: See you there.

This feels normal to most men. It's not how we have all of our conversations, but when our aim is to see someone, it's how the conversation might proceed. It's not all that different from how you might schedule a meeting at work.

This is not how most women talk to each other or how they want to talk to men.

For one thing, most women hate making plans for more than a day or two in the future. This applies particularly to younger women, many of whom won't want to commit themselves in advance to specific plans. What if something more exciting comes up? What if she doesn't feel like it when that day rolls around? How is she supposed to remember what she's supposed to be doing in a few days anyway? (If you run into this problem, it provides a convincing clue that the date is more important to you than it is to her. If her favorite band was playing next week, she'd remember.) If you make long-term plans with a woman who doesn't usually organize her social life like this, you are just asking for her to say "call me to confirm" as if your date was a 1980s-era airplane reservation that could be cancelled without notice.

"Call me to confirm" is a great maneuver for women and I have to admire its cleverness. Now she's locked you into plans if she wants them. She has a date option. She can now decide the day before, or the day of, if this is in fact what she wants to do or whether she'd prefer to do something else, knowing that you've kept that slot open for her. This is even better for her than making firm plans and then cancelling, because she knows that most men, even orbiters (see Glossary), won't stand for endless cancellations. But men will generally tolerate a few occasions when plans "fall through," especially if they were never confirmed in the first place.

Alright, enough about what not to do. Here's how to do it right.

Phone Game: Early

Call her (or send a text message)[9] soon after meeting her for the first time. Contact her that day, if you like, or the following day.

In the first call, you will probably have to do most of the talking, at least for the first minute or two. Call to tell her about something funny that happened, or to ask her a question. Whatever you do, you have to seize her attention. Your first call with a woman should never go like this:

> *Her: Hello?*
>
> *You: Hi, is Julie there?*
>
> *Her: This is Julie.*
>
> *You: Hi, it's Dave. We met at Balboa Park yesterday.*
>
> *Her: Oh, yeah. Hi.*
>
> *You: How's it going?*
>
> *Her: Not bad, you?*
>
> *You: Not bad.*

You've just lost the first eight lines of dialogue – the most important eight lines – dissipating any emotional momentum (see Chapter 4) your first interaction with her could possibly have created. You've brought the energy level down when you needed to raise it up.

Why up? Consider her emotional state. When you met her, she was out, she was probably being social, and she was probably having a good time. In that emotional

---

[9] *Also known as SMS in various parts of the world. Most cellphones have the capability to send and receive short text messages, and that is what we are referring to here. Some women, especially younger women, are obsessed with text messages. Try text or phone or both.*

state, she was interested enough in you to give you her phone number. Now, when you're calling her again, you're calling on your timetable, but not necessarily hers. She may no longer be feeling social and happy and interested in meeting people. She might be miserable or tired or stressed. You need to quickly get her back to how she felt when you met her, while knowing nothing about her current emotional state.

This is why we use callback humor and also take command of the conversation early, to give ourselves an opportunity to put her in a receptive emotional state.

Contrast the bad conversation beginning above to this one:

> Her: Hello?
>
> You: Hey, crazy redhead bodyguard [or whatever piece of callback humor is relevant]... the craziest thing just happened, I just got back from the gym and I met someone who looked just like you.
>
> Her: Oh yeah?
>
> You: Yeah, so do you have a twin sister I should know about? I mean, one of you in the world I could deal with, but two of you would be too much for one planet. What are we going to do about this? [playful tone]

Notice that you don't ask her what she's doing or how she is. Those questions give her an easy excuse to give reasons why she can't be on the phone.

Voicemail

If you get her voicemail, either she didn't get to her phone in time, or she saw your number and didn't feel like talking to you at that moment. You did program your name into her phone, right?

Well, leave her a message! Make it a "call to action" message. You want her to return the call. Examples of elements that incorporate a call to action include:

- I didn't know you knew my friend Kelly.

- My friend said that you... [hang up on yourself]

- Oh my God, you'll never guess what just happened.

Obviously, pick something that's true and that you can be congruent with.

By the way, if you phone, and it goes directly to voicemail (and doesn't ring at all), hang up. You got a free pass. If it doesn't ring, it won't show up as a missed call on her phone, and she won't see that you called. If it does ring, leave a message.

If you don't like your message as you are recording it, try hitting the * or the # key. Often that will give you the opportunity to erase and re-record the message. Don't count on this though, and don't do what I did a few years ago which was end a message by saying "Oh, this sounds really stupid, I'm going to do it again" before hitting the key. It was the wrong key and the message saved automatically. She never called back. Live and learn.

Phone Game: Middle

Now that you've got a conversation going, you want to get her to meet up with you, right? Well, maybe. On the first call, I usually don't.

With enough intuition and practice, you'll be able to judge the right moment to suggest plans. As long as you are doing good work building comfort on the phone, there is no rush. Usually, in fact, a woman will start dropping hints that she wants to meet, especially if you talk about the fun activities and friends that you experience in your day-to-day life. This can happen on the first, second, or even a subsequent call.

The reason for this caution is that you definitely do not want her to say no to potential plans. In case you were wondering, her being busy is a "no." Even if she is genuinely busy, the fact that she is saying no to you affects her perception of your relationship. It also costs you emotional momentum. If you keep pursuing her while she is saying no, you can turn yourself into an orbiter and she will lose all attraction for you. To counteract this, frame your suggested plans in such a way as to minimize the impact of rejection. For example, if you text a woman to say "Hey all, big party at the House of Blues tonight, use my name at the door," you lose very little by a rejection. It's a text message that's framed to look like a group text message, which is technically not an invite to a date. You actually get a bit of value from this whether she shows up or not because it shows you are leading an interesting life and having fun with or without her.

Even more traditional date invitations should not be open-ended. Let's say it's Sunday and you want to see this woman sometime this week. You don't call her and say, "I'd like to see you. Are you free tomorrow? No? How about Tuesday? Ok, Wednesday then? Well, what are you doing Thursday? Friday? Ok, I'll call you next week and see what your schedule looks like then." By doing this, you communicate that you have nothing going on in your life, or at least nothing that is more important than a date with her.

> Women are looking to share their lives with a man. It's not particularly compelling for a woman to share her life with a man when she is the most interesting thing going on in it.

Spontaneity is your friend. If you call a woman at 5 p.m. on a weekday, talk for a couple of minutes, and "spontaneously" ask what she's doing, then this can be seen two ways. It can be seen as an invitation to make plans or just idle conversation. If what she's doing is driving to her cousin's house to baby-sit, then you tell her what you're doing tonight. Try to make it something you probably couldn't invite her to anyway; no plans suggested = no plans rejected. If she instead answers, "Not much," then you can suggest something. She's less likely to cancel if the plans are for the same day.

If you do get rejected for more formal plans (or she cancel at the last minute) you should generally not suggest plans again until after a few more calls. But don't let the conversation end on this note. Quickly change the subject to a high-impact funny or exciting story (which you should have cued up beforehand) and continue the conversation for at least another few minutes.

Phone Game: End

Aim for 12-25 minute conversations and make sure you get off the phone first. You can demonstrate value in doing so by having another call you need to take, or your friend just showed up to take you to some high-status event, or something similar. If you want to refresh her attraction to you, you can demonstrate that you are a Challenge by, for example, telling her you'll call her back in an hour and not doing so.

If she is busy, at work or being distracted, just say "I'll call you back when you're not distracted." If she tries to get you to stay on the phone, then stay, unless the distraction is really annoying.

Phone Game Outside of Comfort

Sometimes for whatever reason you weren't able to follow the preferred technique of getting to the Comfort phase before getting her phone number. Usually in this situation she won't answer when you call, but sometimes she will. If you're in this situation, you need to finish the Attraction and Qualification phases at the same time, and count of having more and longer phone calls.

One way of qualifying when you are in phone game is to make plans with her – even if you know there is no way she is going to show up – and then cancel them later. The plans can be tentative if they have to be, but the cancellation has to be specific. "We should go to this concert next Friday, I'll call you next week about it" is unlikely to rejected by most women. Next Friday is still likely an abstract concept to her, and she likes having many social options for a given night. Saying yes to this spares her the social awkwardness of having to say no. When the time comes, of course, she will probably not answer your call, or send you a text message that she "has to work" or "isn't feeling well" or "has to pick up her sister at the airport." But for now, she's said, "Yes, call me next week."

Treat this as rock-solid formal plans and then cancel on her before she can cancel on you. Call her the night before or the day of and explain (to her voicemail if you have to) that you can't make it because your friend Alexandra is flying out the next day and you totally forgot, but you're hosting a party for her. Don't offer to reschedule or anything.

Call her again in a day or two and continue as normal.

If she doesn't call you back

If she doesn't call back, try her again in a couple days. Or try sending her a text message. Or try calling from a different phone number. Don't use "call block" to hide your phone number when you call her. That's lame.

Some women are just busy or unable to organize their lives or have strange ideas about the appropriateness of calling men, or are deliberately screening for men who are persistent. Unless she's going to tell other people with whom you're likely to interact that you're a creep, it's okay to keep calling or texting a few times to try to make contact. You never know what is going on in her head, and it only costs you 30 seconds to call. Here are some more things you can do to get a woman on the phone:

- Vary the time of day when you call. Morning, afternoon, evening, night. If you're getting nowhere, try calling at midnight. You may wake her up, so make sure you can be immediately entertaining from the second she answers. (Start with a high-energy, funny, short routine. Don't even introduce yourself.)

- Keep old phone numbers around. Holidays can be a great occasion for women to come out of the woodwork. Texting every woman in your phone book with something like "Happy New Year" can sometimes reconnect you with a couple of them.

- Don't ever acknowledge that you are calling and she isn't returning your calls. Adopt the frame - to yourself - that she is just a flaky woman and it's kind of cute. Don't let it cross your mind that she might not actually be interested in you. Therefore, don't ever say "this is the last time I'm calling" or "I'm calling to leave you another message."

Finally, there's the Greatest Text Message Ever™. Send her the text message: "I just met your twin." This may not only jar her into responding, but may prompt her to compete for your affection with a response like "is she prettier than me?" or "I'm cooler."

Flaking

Flaking means canceling plans at the last minute, or not showing up. Guess what? This will happen sometimes, especially on first dates. It's in the nature of things. Here's what to do when a woman flakes:

Nothing.

And that's it.

What, you miss my bullet points? What's Magic Bullets without bullet points? Fine. Here's the same answer, in four bullet points.

- Don't be upset. Don't lecture her. She doesn't care. If she cared that much about what you thought of her, she probably wouldn't have flaked in the first place. Don't believe me? Ask yourself if "feeling tired" or "having to work in the morning" would have kept her from a date with Brad Pitt. All that punishing her will do is to associate yourself in her mind with bad emotions, and momentarily make her feel badly. But don't worry, she'll feel better when the next guy gives her attention.

- Just in case that wasn't clear... You planned to meet her at 6 p.m.? You had to leave work early? Fight traffic? Cut your workout short? Miss your favorite show? Tough. She doesn't care. That's not her problem. If you tell her all of this, you just lost value in her eyes because you rearranged your life for a date with her.

- Remember Pre-selection (Chapter 3) and act like a man who has lots of women interested in him. Such a man wouldn't be especially thrown off by a flake. He has other women in his life who would love to see him, and more likely than not, whatever it was that he was going to do with her was something that he would enjoy doing anyway with cool friends (see Chapter 16 on dates). If this frame is not perfectly clear and obvious to you, cancel the next time you set up a date with a random woman. I'm serious. Listen for her reaction and learn to copy it. It didn't ruin her day. It shouldn't ruin yours.

- A phrase I've had a lot of success with is "No problem, I'll invite someone else." This is best used when your plans were obviously for two people (e.g., you had two concert tickets and invited her). Don't use this on a third or fourth date, but when the relationship is still casual, it's perfect.

Appendix

Chapter 23: Glossary

All-female or all-woman group
A group of people interacting with each other that is made up entirely of women.

Approaching
Initiating a conversation with a woman or a group. Also known as Opening.

Approach Anxiety
The feeling of nervousness most men experience before approaching a woman they don't hknow.

Approach Invitation
Conscious or subconscious behavior a woman exhibits to let a man know that she is interested in having him approach her. Examples include making eye contact or walking or standing near him.

Cold Approach
Approaching a woman (or a group) whom you don't know. Distinguished from Warm Approach, where you have some connection with the woman you approach.

Congruence
Consistency of behavior to identity. If you display personality trait X, congruence requires you act in' a manner consistent with someone with that personality trait.

DHV
Demonstration of Higher Value. Also used as a verb, to Demonstrate Higher Value. This refers to having more value than most men who meet women through cold approach.

Disqualifier
Something you say or do that implies that you are not romantically or sexually interested in a woman.

Embedding

The process of communicating something, usually positive qualities about yourself, in the context of appearing to be talking about something else.

Emotional Momentum

The psychological process carrying you and a woman forward in a potential romantic or sexual relationship or away from each other and further romantic or sexual contact.

Evolutionary Time

The hundreds of thousands of years of human history during which our genetic makeup was formed.

Flake

When a woman cancels plans at the last minute, or does not show up.

Frame

The context under which an interaction takes place. If a woman touches you and you playfully remove her hand and say "no touching this early," your frame is that she is trying to get physical with you. Her frame may be entirely different. The dominant person's frame will usually take precedence.

Group

Two or more people interacting with each other. Two friends going to dinner are a group of two. Three women at a bar that are being hit on by three men are a group of six.

Let's Just Be Friends zone (LJBF)

When a woman has mentally written you off as a potential romantic or sexual partner.

Mixed group

A group of people interacting with each other that includes both men and women.

Normal Conversation	A normal conversation is one that can range freely over a variety of topics, including personal ones.
Opener	A way to start a conversation with a woman or group.
Opening	Approaching a woman or women without awkwardness and smoothly starting a conversation.
Orbiter	Many women get psychological satisfaction out of having men in their social circle who consistently desire her, even if she is unattainable for them. We call these men orbiters. In addition to friendship, these men provide attention, protection, companionship, and ego-validation.
Rooting	Mentioning specific details that make a situation more real and less abstract. Often used in opinion openers (see Chapter 5) and occasionally in story-telling (Chapter 17).
Sexual behavior	Touching that goes beyond kissing.
Sexual Situation	A sexual situation is one in which she is engaging in sexual behavior (beyond kissing) with you, in a place where sex could realistically happen.
Social Circle	Your network of friends, colleagues, and acquaintances, their friends and acquaintances, etc.
State Break	An interruption of what is transpiring in a way that is susceptible to engaging her logical brain.
Value (male)	How desirable you are to a given woman based on what she's learned about you.

Value (female)

A woman's perception of how desirable she is to men in general.

Chapter 24: Resources

This book is a great tool, and will provide you with a strong foundation for improving your skills and bolstering your confidence with women. With the knowledge gleaned from these pages and lots of practice, you will see a marked improvement in your interactions with women.

However, not everything can be taught in one book. Some techniques are hard to convey on the written page, and others are far too advanced for general consumption. For that reason, we've compiled a list of further resources that can help you achieve even more.

In general, these are the things you should be considering for improving your skills after reading this book:

1. Workshops and training

2. Advanced material

3. Routines

4. Keeping up to date

Workshops and training

You can read about it, see it, and hear it, but there's really no substitute for actually doing it.

Live training usually involves three things:

- Intensive classroom seminars, with individualized feedback on your fashion, identity, routines, and rigorous drills and exercises to practice opening and approaching, storytelling, qualification, and so on. You will be prepared and ready to succeed from the first night.

- Approaching and attempting to seduce random beautiful women, over and over, anywhere from coffee shops to bars. A professional dating coach will watch and listen and tell you after each approach what you did right and wrong and how to improve for the next one. And you'll keep doing it until you improve.

- Watching and listening to a master dating coach at work, as he demonstrates various techniques and gives you behaviors and strategies to model. You can see how a master dating coach can attract even the most unapproachable women – live. This is important. If you don't know what solid game really looks like, it's very hard to develop it for yourself.

Love Systems workshops (www.lovesystems.com/bootcamps) include 3 days of seminar work, 2 nights of field work (where you and the instructors go out to meet and practice on beautiful women), and a money-back guarantee. As someone familiar with Magic Bullets, you will be well-placed to take advantage of a workshop.

Love Systems also offers individualized or one-on-one training. This is more expensive, but may be more convenient for some people.

It's easy to postpone attending a workshop. They're not cheap and they're not always convenient. We can say with confidence that this is a mistake. On your first day of the workshop, you will probably be blown away by the instructors' skills. Don't be. They were once in your chair. If you learn from them and practice what you've learned, your skills can equal or exceed theirs. We've seen this happen over and over; that's how Love Systems recruits new instructors.

There's never a perfect time to take a workshop. There's always a reason not to. Part of dating science is internal transformation, and that includes seizing the moment. If you're serious about having beautiful women as a normal and easy part of your life, then make it happen. Now. Waiting a year just means that you will have one year less to enjoy your new skills once you develop them. You don't get extra time at the end to enjoy your life just because you were late getting started.

Another pitfall some people fall into is waiting to take a workshop until their skills improve. This is backward. The progress people make after a workshop is infinitely quicker than the progress they made before one. And you should have the results you want now, or in a few months, as opposed to some distant future point.

Once you've read this book, start planning your workshop now. Pick a date. Sign up. Pay your deposit. Make it happen for real.

Selected advanced material

By far the best source of advanced material is a monthly audio program creatively known as The Interview Series. Every month, two of the world's top dating coaches are interviewed together on a specific subject, ranging from Approaching to Seduction, from Phone Game to Threesomes. It's a unique product, since every topic gets treated in tremendous depth, from at least two perspectives, and there's an opportunity to hear the tonality and delivery that the masters use in different situations.

We strongly recommend subscribing to the interview series at:
www.LoveSystems.com/ivs. It's $24.99 per month plus shipping.

When you subscribe, you will be sent the current month's interview, and a new interview every month afterward. So you don't have to start back at CD#1, but all of the previous interviews do make an excellent home study library for an amazing number of different topics.

That being said, it's much cheaper to subscribe (about 50% off). Plus subscribers get the interviews usually several months before everyone else, and other goodies including their own mailing list and bonus content.

Other than attending a live workshop, this is the single most important thing you can do right now:

www.LoveSystems.com/ivs

Advanced material, by topic

In this section, we've combined all of the previous interviews with some other resources we recommend, and sorted them by topic. For anything you are having trouble with or want to improve, you can go straight to the source.

Learning Game:

Mr. M and Rokker on the Right Way to Learn Game:
(www.lovesystems.com/cd17)

Braddock, Rokker, and Mr. M on Sticking Points:
(www.lovesystems.com/cd27)

Approaching and Transitioning:

Sinn and Savoy on Opening (www.lovesystems.com/cd1)

The Don and Tenmagnet on The First Five Minutes (www.lovesystems.com/cd14)

Attraction:

Future and Tenmagnet on Value (www.lovesystems.com/cd16)

Braddock and Dahunter on Teasing (www.lovesystems.com/cd30)

Cajun and Tenmagnet on Role Plays (www.lovesystems.com/cd32)

Qualification:

Sinn and Vision on Qualification (www.lovesystems.com/cd8)

Mr. M, Braddock, and Sphinx on Issues in Qualification
(www.lovesystems.com/cd37)

Seduction:

Sinn and Tenmagnet on Seduction (www.lovesystems.com/cd12)

Soul and Johnny Wolf on Logistics: Taking Her Home
(www.lovesystems.com/cd33)

Braddock and Kisser on Turning Things Sexual (www.lovesystems.com/cd40)

Relationships:

Relationship Management DVDs from Savoy
(www.lovesystems.com/relationship-management)

Meeting women in bars and clubs:

Savoy and The Don on Advanced Winging (www.lovesystems.com/cd21)

Moxie and Future on Obstacles and Other Men (www.lovesystems.com/cd7)

Savoy and The Don on Cold Reads (www.lovesystems.com/cd23)

Mr. M and Sheriff on High-End Club Game (www.lovesystems.com/cd28)

Meeting women outside of bars and clubs:

Savoy and Tenmagnet on Warm Approach (www.lovesystems.com/cd13)

Savoy and Badboy on Social Circles (www.lovesystems.com/cd20)

Day Game Workshop (www.lovesystems.com/daygame)

Social Circle Mastery seminar (www.lovesystems.com/social-circle)

Humor:

Sinn and Future on Storytelling (www.lovesystems.com/cd3)

Braddock and Cajun on Humor (www.lovesystems.com/cd35)

Mainstream humor books and DVDs that have been recommended by past students:

- Humor Theory: Formula of Laughter by Igor Krichtafovitch

- True and False: Heresy and Common Sense for the Actor by David Mamet

- Three Uses of the Knife by David Mamet

- Comedian (movie) by Jerry Seinfeld

Female Psychology

Savoy and Soul on Female Psychology (www.lovesystems.com/cd34)

Phone Game:

Sinn and Savoy on Phone Game (www.lovesystems.com/cd10)

Dates:

Ajax and Future on Dates (www.lovesystems.com/cd4)

Fashion and identity:

Tenmagnet, Sinn, and Future on Identity (www.lovesystems.com/cd6)

Moxie and Savoy on Being In State (www.lovesystems.com/cd29)

Big Business and Prestige on Love Systems in Everyday Life
(www.lovesystems.com/cd36)

Inner Game seminar (www.lovesystems.com/inner-game)

Advanced Strategies:

Sinn and Savoy on Frame Control (www.lovesystems.com/cd5)

Savoy and Brad P. on Taking Chances (www.lovesystems.com/cd15)

Sinn and The Don on Physical Escalation and Kissing
(www.lovesystems.com/cd11)

Savoy and Speer on Damage Control
(www.lovesystems.com/cd22)

The Don and Savoy on Using and Creating Routines (www.lovesystems.com/cd9)

Tenmagnet, Braddock, and Cajun on Jealousy Plotlines
(www.lovesystems.com/cd24)

Braddock, Mr. M, and Sheriff on How to Be an Alpha Male
(www.lovesystems.com/cd25)

Soul, Badboy, and Cortez on Direct Game
(www.lovesystems.com/cd26)

Braddock and Mr. M on 9 and 10 Game (www.lovesystems.com/cd31)

Soul and Kisser on Handling Tests (www.lovesystems.com/cd38)

Savoy and Kisser on Older Men Dating Younger Women
(www.lovesystems.com/cd39)

One night stands:

One Night Stands seminar (www.lovesystems.com/ons)

Threesomes:

Savoy and Badboy on Threesomes (www.lovesystems.com/cd18)

Strippers and Hired Guns:

Strippers and Hired Guns seminar (www.lovesystems.com/strippers)

Routines Manual

The Routines Manual is the biggest new product to hit the dating community in years. Written by Love Systems instructor The Don, the book provides hundreds of routines created and tested by top professionals in the field.

The book is divided up by the phases of the Emotional Progression Model, and explains what kinds of rou-tines are appropriate for each. Finally, there's an advanced section on how to make your own routines, as well as a further discussion of storytelling. Feel confident and never run out of things to say again! For information and to purchase the Routines Manual, visit www.LoveSystems.com/Routines. There are also free sample chapters available on that page that you can read right now.

Once you've mastered the awesome material in the Routines Manual Volume 1, you may be ready for the Love Systems Routines Manual Volume 2! Featuring all-new scripts and routines for every phase of the interaction, Volume 2 also has bonus chapters on day game, phone and text game, and cold reads. Even that's not all. Volume 2 even has the first printing of Love Systems' all-new Triad model, the next evolutionary leap of the Emotional Progression Model. For more information and to purchase the Routines Manual Volume 2, visit:

www.LoveSystems.com/Routines-Manual-2.

Keep up to date

The best way to keep up to date with new developments in dating science is of course to subscribe to the Interview Series (www.LoveSystems.com/ivs). But that's not the only source of continuing information and resources. In fact, there are three good places to check out.

The Attraction Forums (www.theattractionforums.com). This phenomenal website is a great place to find a "wingman," to search for and read articles and "field reports" from the masters, to share information and ask questions to others, to find or post routines, and to make friends. It's free.

The Love Systems Publications Library: (www.lovesystems.com/publications). Many of the best techniques and field reports are added to this library, which grows every week. It's a great database for the best tips to develop your skills.

The Love Systems Instructors' Blog (blog.lovesystems.com). Listen in as our top instructors discuss their bootcamps, new techniques, and humorous anecdotes from real in-field experiences.

You will also want to check out our free newsletter, the Love Systems Insider (LSi). It's full of great informa-tion and new breakthroughs, and reading it regularly will inspire you to keep developing your skills. You can join (for free!) at the signup box on our homepage or go directly to www.lovesystems.com/LSi.

Conclusion

Not every good resource is listed here. However, this should give you a road map for future development. We were once in your shoes, so we know what it's like. Write us any time at info@LoveSystems.com.

Chapter 25: Reviews and Testimonials

Here are just a few of the thousands of positive comments, reviews, and testimonials garnered by Magic Bullets:

"To put it simply, the book is a wonderful piece of work. I highly recommend it to all beginners who wish to learn the steps to becoming great at the art... From your approach to seduction everything is mapped out to the 'letter' with more than enough freedom for the imagination to run wild. As with most technology in this day and age, if Magic Bullets were a computer program I would call it very 'user friendly.' I found it extremely helpful to have a book like this bring me back into the dating 'shark tank' as the shark instead of the bait. My advice to all is to get this book and let it do the same for you."

— Nostro

"Magic Bullets is one of the best books ever written on the subject of improving success with women. It's probably one of the most honest, well rounded, information-packed books you will read. One unique aspect of Magic Bullets that sets it apart is each chapter is written in logical order, but can be read on its own even without reading the others. This is great because you can just review those chapters that you need to refresh separately. Or for example, if you are a beginner and want a quick primer on what will help you in clubs tonight, there is a chapter that will do that for you that you can skip to right away."

"Another thing that was extremely impressive about the book was just how in-depth and well researched it was and yet it still included very subtle advice at the same time. The book was full of deep, masterful detail in every chapter. One of my favorite things about this book was the extreme level of detail in the Seduction phase, which is definitely lacking in most books of its type. In the book you get some real 'magic bullets' on how to get to sex faster and with higher probability of success. These tips and gems alone are well worth the price of the book."

"For those looking for very niche and advanced material, there is no shortage of that either. The book is truly well rounded for beginners and veteran students of the game alike. Whether you are a beginner or an advanced student of the arts, you owe it to yourself to begin your education with this book or add it to your collection. The information contained in it is state of the art and hard hitting. Get your copy now, and start enjoying your own magic results with women.
When I first 'met' Savoy it was actually over the phone over a distance of thousands of miles, and at the time I had no idea he knew so much about seduction. In the years that have ensued, it is clear to me from meeting him in person finally and

reading Magic Bullets that Savoy has become even more knowledgeable and one of the true experts in the field."

— TokyoPUA , Fast Seduction 101

"Magic Bullets fills in some knowledge gaps, often in very important areas, it gives you an 'aha!'"

"Now for intermediate to advanced guys, I think this book fills in some very important specific knowledge gaps... The section on phone game is a great example of this. What exactly do you do when you hit her voicemail anyway? The great Tyler Durden himself said that phone game was hard just starting from first principles. In Magic Bullets we can see that a ton of work has gone into presenting solid phone game strategy."

"Also, the discussion on flaking was excellent. It nicely summarizes what it took me forever to learn by raw experimentation: if she flakes, do nothing about it. The book presents a solid model of why to do nothing, namely because she just did not care enough about the whole matter to begin with. Proof: if she did care she wouldn't have flaked! This is typical of great specific, practical, and concise advice that the book is made of."

— Philosopherking

"Magic Bullets gives you a system you can use the same day, without reading the whole book. No other book can beat that. No book gives you a plan in 10 minutes of reading of what you can do that night. Unlike a lot of pickup material, this book touches on female psychology. This chapter was my favorite, second to phone game. The insight you will gain from phone game is worth the price right there. Magic Bullets includes the ever popular 'he said/she said' teaching examples. Every chapter in this book is important. The night I ordered it I read the entire thing. Even though I was tired, I took a NoDoz because I was so determined to finish it and not miss anything because of my fatigue. Everyone who hasn't yet bought Magic Bullets... stop thinking about it and just do it... the price of the book was worth it after just a few pages."

"If I haven't convinced you yet, know this: Savoy does a great job at teaching this material. The format of the book is designed so you can go back and read a chapter on phone game or the Qualification phase. I even e-mailed Savoy with a question about the book and got a prompt response. It's not every day you can ask the author a question and get an answer, especially with someone as busy as he is."

— Surefire

"Magic Bullets does a fine job breaking down the seduction process from meeting women all the way to relationships. It does so while unifying pretty much every 'system' out there, be it indirect, direct, natural routines, phone game, social circles, strip clubs, day game, body language etc. via the emotional progression model. All in all, it was a very informative and entertaining read. It taught me a couple of cool concepts that helped clear up a lot of aspects in pickup that were still pretty vague."

— Toy Machine

"It was a long hard road to admit to myself that I needed to get this part of my life sorted out. I searched the web for a long time seeking a solution to my problem. I wasted a lot of money on 'gurus' only to find myself back reading Magic Bullets. I was hesitant at first but after seeing the money back guarantee I decided to go for it. I read it in 4 hours straight, going back over sentences four times to sink them into my brain. After finishing it, I decided to go and try it. That was the hardest part. I did it and I got my first phone number after almost 2 years! So I got the number and now it's been 4 months since I bought Magic Bullets, and I have to say I'm so much better now. I have a girlfriend, and things are perfect."

— Jan

"It definitely made a huge difference, especially in my second week after reading the book. The improvement was dramatic."

"Stunning! My success in meeting new women went up dramatically the first night."
"I was frankly skeptical at first, but after a week I found myself taking home women who I normally would have been admiring from a distance. Also the seduction tips improved my effectiveness after I got them back to my place."

— Brink Magazine

"Magic Bullets is a leader in the seduction community and learning how to pick up, date, and have more women in your life for a reason. It works. Thousands of guys have gone from being frozen stone-cold in approaching a woman to being 'the man' in a nightclub and even during the day. I highly recommend you grab your copy now!"

— Earthling Communication

"The techniques in the book are practical and easy to use, and you can start using what you learn right away. We really cannot recommend this book enough. Magic Bullets is an essential must read for any man aspiring to be better with women, no matter where you're at in the dating game."

— Sexual Seduction Secrets

"I'd like to say that this is probably the best e-book online at the moment. If you're just starting out, this will be the book to learn 'the game' from start to finish. If you're an old pro, this is a handy reference manual to help you refine the game you already have."

— The Seduction Bible

"I have found Magic Bullets to be extraordinarily useful. Look forward to cover most of what you need to know and most of your blind spots too. Magic Bullets is going to help most men establish their first steps on their social adventure and yet they'll also be able to refer back to reinforce their basics. A guaranteed book to pick up for your pick-ups."."

— MsiaPUA

"It's a great e-book with a great structure... Buy it and you won't be disappointed."

— Slick101

"I will be honest, Magic Bullets is one of the best investments I have made in the field of pickup. This book really explains every little detail of pickup, and I have had a very easy time translating what I have read into what I do. I would say that it is a great investment for a good price."

— salvino

"Magic Bullets is the best. It's the only book that really teaches in a way that is easy to understand and goes right to the chase. It's a guide that you can read over and over again and it also gives you a simple technique that you can read in 10 minutes to apply it the very same day you start reading it! For me it has been most helpful."

— gambalo

"Hey, finished reading Magic Bullets and it's great! You can go back to it whenever you need; you don't even have to read it in order although if you are new to the game then I recommend it."

— Rhyde

"By learning just one new thing from this book, your dating life will improve... "

— squidoo

"This is awesome! It worked. I went to the club yesterday, and I got four phone numbers."

— Brian D.

"The e-book is comprehensive and delivers. Savoy did a great job with his writing, and I recommend this e-book in full."

— m-dawg

"I've always been hopeless at getting women to be interested in me. Well, after I picked up Magic Bullets it was all pistons firing. I now have three dates lined up this week. That's more than in the past 6 months combined."

— Matt

"What do I think of Magic Bullets? Was I expecting it to change my dating life? Maybe. Did it? Yes!"

— Joe

"You really hit the head on the nail with this one mate. I've read heaps of other stuff on the internet but none have given me an outlined plan like yours has. Thanks."

— Andy

"I like how this book is compiled. No fluff, easy to read, straight to the point. Most of the content is presented in short sentences or bullet point format. You can just jump to specific parts of the book like to bolster your understanding before going out. Most of the subchapters take 5-10 minutes to read and you're good to go, no need to read 3 pages of solid text to 'get it.'"

— joule

"You can tell by the professional appearance and the attention to detail that a lot of work was put into making this book a superior product. There are some books that, despite having some decent information, are poorly put together and elicit the feeling that the author wanted to make a quick buck by putting out an e-book as soon as possible. This does not appear to be the case with Magic Bullets."

"The book is called Magic Bullets because the tips in the book are so good that they will seem like magic!"

— Mr. Esquire

"Magic Bullets is beautifully written because it deals with the reader on a few different levels. There's a lot of stuff for newbies, so if you aren't already good, the book is perfect. But even within the newbie-ish stuff, there is a lot of stuff for advanced guys. Often major pearls of wisdom are inside sections that appear at first to be more general.

— Orpheus7

"I love how Magic Bullets is written so that you can browse through the chapters for something specific. Savoy captures the whole concept of 'game' in an easy to understand, easy to follow way. Savoy just refines 'game' in general."

— Beqone

"The way Savoy organized the book is fantastic, and the book is incredibly dense with material. Since I ordered it, I've read it 3 times through with tons of quick readings over specific chapters I had questions about after that particular night's interactions. I highly recommend it."

— rekkless

"Magic Bullets is the only book (e-book or not) on game that is worth the time and money invested in it."

— Rewok

"Savoy masterfully helped me create a personal story and it was mesmerizing to watch him so naturally run game on women in the field."

— Ansan

Thanks to the massive success of Love Systems and the ever-increasing legions of satisfied students,Savoy has been asked to appeare on many radio shows, in newspapers, and on interviews discussingMagic Bullets and his proven techniques. These have included the Dr. Phil Show, Fox News, Playboy TV, Maxim Radio, CBS Radio, 3WT Talk Radio, MSMobiles.com!

"You're giving people the tools to go meet women."

– Dr. Phil Show, April 18, '08

"I'd like to especially say thanks to Savoy for taking the time to work with me both nights. He took over one of my interactions and it really helped to see the dominance/frame control of someone who's good. That alone was worth the whole workshop."

— The Bonus

"Savoy, I wanted to thank you very much for responding to my question about relationship breakups in the latest newsletter. The degree to which you care about your students only further motivates my journey to excellence in life and as a PUA. Love Systems has changed my life and I am very appreciative."

— Puzzler

"I found Savoy a pleasure to work with, very fair, and a talented businessman of the highest integrity. I often say that he could have been extremely successful in any business venture, though he chose to come into an industry that is filled with a variety of eccentric personalities. Within this difficult industry, he put himself on the line to build a company that delivers high quality and whose customer service I've found to be impeccable... I wanted to salute him for all that he has created, the people he has made successful, and his overall fairness, generosity, and integrity. I can always count on Savoy both to listen to and to respect my point of view and also to offer his viewpoint honestly and fairly on any given subject."

— DJ

Room for your Notes: